ACTORS' GUIDE

OTHER BOOKS BY DONALD C. FARBER:

Producing on Broadway: A Comprehensive Guide

From Option to Opening: A Guide for the
Off-Broadway Producer

Financing the Film — *forthcoming*

ACTORS' GUIDE

what you should know about the contracts you sign

by **DONALD C. FARBER**

DRAMA BOOK SPECIALISTS/PUBLISHERS
NEW YORK, NEW YORK

Library of Congress Catalog Card Number: 79-134992

ISBN Book Number: 0910482-19-5

In memory of my father, Charles Farber, and my friends John Emery and Harvey Breit, whose untimely deaths were deeply felt.

TABLE OF CONTENTS

PREFACE

I am very often consulted by an actor or an actress who, having entered into a contract without advice, now needs help to amend, clarify, or break the contract. The job is always easier to do in the first place than to undo in the second place. I always help as best I can and I make a deal with each of them. I promise not to become an actor (if I could), if they promise not to practice law any more (which they do).

With this thought in mind, why should anyone write a book to explain simply and in detail what certain legal documents mean?—for such is the purpose of this book. A short book such as this can hardly equip one with the experience necessary to negotiate contracts effectively and to understand all the complicated legal provisions encompassed in many of the agreements. Nor could I learn to act from reading a similar book on acting.

Most actors and actresses, being creative people, do not know how, cannot, and have no real desire to attend to their business needs. Agents, managers, accountants, and attorneys do this for them. This is perhaps as it should be. Since an actor entering into an agreement with an agent rarely (though it sometimes happens) consults an attorney before signing the mass of papers placed before him, most actors have no idea, or at best a very vague idea, of what the agency agreements mean. It's an even more confusing situation for the actor about to sign a management contract, for the terms, as we will later learn, are most varied and cover a very wide range.

It is also sometimes confusing as to who works for whom. One ought to understand that by the very nature of the legal arrangement, the agent (or manager or attorney) is an "agent," which means that the actor is the "principal." An "agent" acts on behalf of a "principal." The principal does not act on behalf of the agent. If this relationship is kept in mind, one can better understand what the duties and obligations of one to another are all about.

I am not suggesting that there is or is not anything wrong with the agency agreements which are signed. I am saying, however, that actors and actresses, like other professionals, deserve to know what they are doing and what they have done when they enter into such agreements.

Since this book is about contracts, which are sometimes referred to in this book as agreements, we really should have some idea of just what a contract is. The Law Dictionary actually tells us that the word "agreement" is a wider term than "contract" because an agreement, under some circumstances, might not be enforceable because it does not fulfill some legal contract requirement. For our purposes, the words will be used interchangeably, and when I refer to an agreement, I could as well say contract even though the fine legal distinction does exist.

The kinds and classification of contracts is enough to boggle the mind.

A contract is an agreement between two or more persons that creates or modifies a legal relationship. Simply stated, a contract is a legally enforceable agreement.

It is, of course, impossible to become a contract expert by reading this book. The best-known legal treatise on contracts, written by Williston, consists of nine thick volumes. It would be helpful, however, to know that a contract may be oral or written under some circumstances. The Statute of Frauds, which the Legislatures of most States have passed, requires that contracts of certain kinds or under certain circumstances must be in writing to be enforced. If a contract does not come within the Statute of Frauds, then it is enforceable whether it is written or oral. Of course, it is much easier to prove the existence and the terms of the written contract.

To have a contract there must be at least two parties who have a meeting of the minds. Each of the parties obligates himself to do or not to do something. For a contract to be enforceable there must be consideration for the agreement. If someone promises to do something without any consideration, a contract does not exist and the gratuitous promise would not be enforceable. In addition to consideration, in order to have a contract the obligation must be clearly defined. An actor agreeing to perform in a play on evenings that he feels like working would hardly be enforceable.

One should also bear in mind that an agreement to agree

is also unenforceable. For an example, if an actor and a producer agree that the actor will be hired for the road company of the play after the New York production, upon terms to be negotiated between the parties, such an agreement would be unenforceable. Either party need simply demand outrageous terms in the negotiations to prevent an agreement. An effort is sometimes made to put teeth into such a clause by providing that the actor will be hired upon terms to be negotiated between the parties "in good faith." This would raise the question as to whether the parties are negotiating in good faith and, I suspect, there might be some way to have an arbitration or a lawsuit to prove that a party was not negotiating in good faith. I would much rather not have to prove to a court or arbitrator the good faith of a party in negotiations because this is something most difficult to prove.

If you want an enforceable agreement, be sure to make the terms specific and exact, not vague, uncertain or later to be decided. It is sometimes difficult to fix such exact terms but, believe me, it is much less difficult than trying to enforce a contract which is not a binding obligation.

There has developed in the entertainment industry a certain kind of understanding between the people working in the business. It is not unusual for parties to make oral commitments which could not be legally enforced which neither party would think of not living up to. Such commitments, I suspect, could be thought of as moral obligations, but they are more than moral obligations in that, if an attorney, or an agent, or a personal manager did not live up to his oral commitment it would only be a short period of time before many people in the business knew about it. In addition to being marked lousy, the party would not again be trusted, and it is much easier to function in the entertainment industry with people trusting you. These oral commitments are, in most instances, always reduced to writing later.

This book is not intended to replace your attorney's advice or to discourage you from entering into any particular contracts, although it may have that affect. It is intended to simplify and make understandable a large group of legal documents which most actors sign without understanding.

This book will not tell you how to get an agent. It is sometimes said that one may get an agent as one may get a bank loan: when one can prove one doesn't need it. Nor will this book tell you whether you should or should not have an agent or, if so, which one. This book has one purpose—to simplify and clarify certain documents you may sign in the course of your professional career.

A good representative should always be ready to do whatever is best for his client, even if it means giving up some of his interest in the client's earnings. At least three times each day I find my self advising that five percent of something big can be a lot of money and ninety-five percent of nothing is nothing. It sometimes happens that the narrow-sighted personal manager will not part with the small percentage of the client's earnings (either from the client's share or from his own share) that could "make the whole thing happen."

It's impossible for me to discuss representation of performers without some few words about attorneys. Of course the role of an attorney may overlap the role of the agent and manager. It shouldn't, but it often does. All negotiate and prepare contracts, and managers and attorneys may both care for the performer's funds. Some performers prefer to have their attorney handle all these functions, while others prefer to have an attorney and agent both. Some even have an attorney, an agent, and a manager handling all their affairs. Agents and managers (unless they are attorneys—and some are) cannot practice law. True, some large agencies have legal counsel on their staff. It's my experience, however, and this most will admit, that it is impossible for the agency counsel to give the performer's problem the same attention which the performer's own lawyer will give to it.

Agents and attorneys ought to work together when a client has engaged both. For your information, you do not need your agent's consent to engage an attorney. Nor do you need your attorney's consent to engage an agent. Advice is one thing; required consent is another.

For the most part, a writer, actor, director, designer, or other creative person should expect at the very least that his attorney and agent cooperate for his common interest to make the best arrangement possible and to get proper contracts to set forth exactly what the arrangement is. This is what usually happens.

Realize that your agent, your manager, your attorney, and your accountant work for you. You are in charge. You may take their advice if you value such advice. If not, you should get a new representative in whom you do have confidence.

Just as there are twenty-seven (or 35 or 72 or more) actors who do not get each part, there are also boodles of musical groups, singers, and other performers who do not make it. Sadly enough, so much of success in the entertainment industry may depend on being in the right place at the right time and in knowing the right person who can make it happen. What is the right place and the right time can to some extent be helped by the right people, but there is no doubt that in many cases, chance plays an important part. Talent always helps, but unfortunately, by itself it often is not enough.

Now that we have decided that chance plays some part, we must go on to realize that we can give "chance" an assist. It's possible to create situations where the chance is more likely to happen, or more likely to occur.

One must bear in mind that planning a performing career can be of great importance. It may be very wrong to take that big juicy part if the part is all wrong for the particular performer, or if it is too soon in the performer's career.

The performer may be faced with a decision concerning which agent or personal manager to select. This is a lovely problem, for most would-be actors would be happy to have any single agent represent them. The decision may boil down to the large agency, which appears to have many connections, versus the smaller agent, with fewer contacts but a stronger motivation and a greater need to help the performer. The aggressive smaller agent or manager may need the performer's success more than the larger agency which is dependent on no one single performer. But the large agency, if motivated, may have an easier job of making it.

As with most decisions in life, there is no one pat answer as to what is right for all performers. Since our needs vary, the methods of satisfying them must of necessity differ. Performers are individuals with varying problems, varying talents, and they may require different promotion, different treatment. (I refuse to say different "handling"—for although the term is commonly used, I do not wish to reinforce the notion that people are handled; it's things that are handled.)

So what to do? Something must be said for what is, I believe, the most important means of picking associates. Plain and simple, it's intuition. Select someone who believes in you, someone with whom you have rapport, and someone you "intuit" is right for you. Select someone who cares about you and about your career, for your career and your problems are the most important things in the world to you, and unless your representative knows and feels this, he will not do well for you. Select someone who will endeavor to accomplish for you what you need to have accomplished. The selection is part of the "chance" involved and it is, or should be, based on your feelings—your "intuition." Intuit well—it's as important or maybe even more important than how you audition for that part.

ACKNOWLEDGMENTS

I must again express my appreciation and gratitude to my dear, beautiful family for tolerating what happens when a busy compulsive like me decides to write books. So Annie, Patty, and Seth, thank you for all.

There were a few other people who made writing this book a little easier. I do want to express my special thanks to Dale Burg for her secretarial help with the book, and especially for her pleasant attitude in making herself ready at those odd times that I had available to do some of the writing. Thanks also go to my secretary, Sharon Filus, and to Harold Kocin of AFTRA, John McGuire of SAG, and Ken Krezel of Equity.

Ralph Pine at Drama Book Specialists, my Publisher-Editor-Friend, helped me in so many ways that I cannot adequately express. His wife, Jeannie, gets thanks for patiently suffering with us.

I do appreciate the Drama Book Shop. Arthur Seelen—thanks for your distinctive wit and humor. Al Collins—thanks for believing in the Drama Book Shop and in the kind of books that you feel should be published and sold. Dorothy Collins—thanks for believing in Al Collins and for tolerating us all.

INTRODUCTION

There is a difference between a theatrical "agent" and a "manager," sometimes referred to as a "personal manager" or "exclusive manager." There are all kinds of agents and all kinds of managers. This book is concerned with the agreements that agents and managers in the performing arts will enter into with their clients, as well as other standard union-approved employment contracts.

To be an agent, that is, to find employment for someone, one must be licensed by the New York City Department of Licenses. A manager need not be licensed, but a manager should not (I know they sometimes do) find employment for his clients.

The agent, in addition to being licensed by the Department of Licenses, must be franchised by each of the performer unions (or associations). Equity, AFTRA, SAG, and AGVA grant each agent, if qualified, a franchise to represent performers in their respective unions. The franchised agent agrees to certain rules and terms applicable to the performer in each respective union, and an important restriction on the agent is the agreement between the agent and the performer which is approved by each union.

The agent cannot give the performer terms less favorable than those union-approved terms.

The AFM (American Federation of Musicians) and AGMA (American Guild of Musical Artists) also have a collective bargaining agreement which is agreed to by each agent or manager who represents one of their members. AFM and AGMA do not actually issue a franchise to the approved agents or managers, but what they do has the same effect, since no agent or manager may sign an AFM or AGMA member without first having signed the union's basic agreement.

Also, in discussing the AGMA contract later, we will discover that an unlicensed manager may find an "engagement" as distinguished from finding a "job" for a client.

Since personal managers are neither licensed nor franchised, they may make any kind of agreement with the performer as long as it is not illegal. I was tempted to say as long as it is not illegal or immoral, but such is not the case. Some management contracts almost approach (and some even achieve) the immoral. Please, I must not be misquoted or misread. By and large *most* agents and *most* managers are both legal and moral with respect to their clients.

The union agency agreement entered into by a performer is a result of collective bargaining by the union with the agents, and the actor is protected to the extent that he cannot be given an agency agreement with terms that are less beneficial than those agreed upon by the respective unions. The union agency agreements include Actors Equity Association, the American Federation of Radio and

Television Artists (AFTRA), two Screen Actors Guild (SAG) agreements, the American Federation of Musicians (AFM), the American Guild of Musical Artists (AGMA), and the American Guild of Variety Artists (AGVA) contract.

Bear in mind also that this book not only discusses union-approved contractual agreements between you and your agent and contractual agreements between you and your manager, but also discusses union contractual agreements of employment which apply to you whether or not you are represented by an agent or manager.

The first part of the book discusses the union-approved agreements between the agent and performer, and the latter part of the book discusses the union agreements of employment between the performer and an employer.

Most talent agencies, especially the larger ones, wish to represent a client in other ways not covered by the standard union-approved agreements and in areas where the standard union-approved agreements are not applicable. For example, an actor may become quite famous as the result of, or in spite of, his agent's representation; however, in either event, as a result of his fame and fortune he may go on to writing magazine articles which might be published throughout the world. The agent would of course like to represent the actor in all endeavors, especially if his fame on the stage is a result of the agent's efforts.

Hence, there are a number of what I will refer to as "catchall" contracts which are intended by the agent to cover everything not covered by the various union-approved agreements. Catchall agreements will be discussed in some detail later.

When the agent prepares the agency agreements for you to sign, he has in mind tying you up in as many ways as possible. That's what it's all about. Actually, there's something to be said for the argument that if the agent makes you famous, and as a result of your fame all kinds of nice things happen, then he should be entitled to share in all the monies received by you as a result of his initial efforts.

The problem that I have is not with the agent's motive, reason, or justification for doing this. The problem that I have is that in doing it, you may be asked to sign agreements, prepared by the agent's legal counsel with great skill and dexterity, with the intention of tying up everything you might do or hope to do in every possible way in the entertainment, literary, and related fields; and in doing this, you may be asked to sign a contract with provisions so ambiguous that on its face it appears to mean something which upon reflection one would realize it should not mean. The language is so broad in some of these agreements that if taken literally, they would seem to provide that the agent could charge commissions on anything you may create, no matter when sold, no matter to whom or what or how it was sold, and no matter when you received compensation for it.

Since, most generally, persons signing agency contracts are not represented by counsel—and even when they are, it's somewhat difficult to get the standard printed agency contract forms changed without a big hassle—it would seem to be incumbent upon the agent to use language in the agency agreements which clearly delineates the areas of representation, the areas in which the agent is entitled to be paid, and length of time of the agreements, as well as setting forth definitively just what the agent is entitled to receive a commission for. In some agency agreements, I must humbly suggest that the very technical legal language used leaves much to be desired.

The actor is usually requested by the agent to sign the following contracts:

Exclusive Management Contract as an actor (Equity)
Standard AFTRA Exclusive Contract (AFTRA)
Theatrical Motion Picture Contract (SAG)
Television Motion Picture Agency Contract (SAG)
AFM Exclusive Agent Musician Agreement (AFM)
Artists Management Contract (AFMA)
Exclusive Agency Contract (AGVA)

You may also be asked to sign several other agreements sometimes variously labeled as follows:

General Services Contract
General Materials and Packages
Industrial Films Agreement
Motion Picture Packages
Packages Representation

Upon careful examination, it may be seen that some of the agency contracts have a good deal in common. In particular, the Actors Equity agreement, the AFTRA agreement, the SAG motion picture agreements covering

| 23

theatrical motion pictures and television motion pictures, as well as the AGVA contract, share many common provisions. All provide that the contract is applicable to a specific part of the entertainment industry. The agent's role is defined. Each sets forth what the agent should do on behalf of the actor, albeit the terms are given in very general language.

More specifically, these agreements contain the following provisions:

1. The contract will provide that the agent represents you exclusively. Exclusive representation means that no one else may represent you in the area covered, and if you get employment in the field in which the agent represents you, he will be reimbursed whether he assisted with the employment or not.

2. The contract will state the terms of the agreement, which the agent will make as long as permitted, usually not in excess of three years.

3. The contract will state what percentage of your earnings is to be retained by the agent as his commission. This is usually not in excess of ten percent, but may be more under certain circumstances.

4. The contract will state that either party may terminate the contract if you are not employed for a certain length of time during a certain period.

5. The contract will very generally and very broadly outline the duties of the agent.

6. The contract will limit certain of your activities.

7. The contract will state the names of specific people in the agency to whom you may look for assistance.

8. There will probably be an arbitration clause of some kind to speed decisions in case of a dispute.

An arbitration clause will provide that instead of a trial or other court proceeding, in the event of a dispute, the parties must settle their differences by submitting the grievance to an arbitrator or arbitrators. The agreement may provide that this be done in accordance with the rules of the American Arbitration Association or in accordance with other procedures outlined in the agreement.

I firmly believe an arbitration clause most desirable, in fact, a must in an agreement covering the entertainment industry. There are many "legal type" lawyers who may differ with me on this viewpoint. For the most part, they are not theatre-oriented, and are more concerned with words than with accomplishing a result for the client.

Arbitration is most desirable in theatrical disputes because:

1. It is fast. *Speed is essential in our business.* Can you imagine the producer who has $750,000 invested in a big musical being confronted by the composer, who will not consent to replacing a disastrously bad choreographer after three weeks of rehearsal? To wait four or five months or several years for a court to decide whether or not the

composer's consent was unreasonably withheld should be unnecessary. Some contracts will specifically authorize and set forth a procedure for a "quick arbitration" in which a decision may be obtained within 24 hours.

Speed is essential as well in determining disputes between an agent and an actor. If an actor claims a breach of the agreement by the agent, it would be advantageous to have the dispute settled in a few months by an arbitrator, rather than in a few years by a judge, so that an actor may know whether the agent will continue to represent him and under what terms and conditions.

2. Arbitrators who know the business can be selected. The list of arbitrators from whom the selection is made consists of people who know and work in the entertainment industry. If the dispute concerns television, one may select an arbitrator who works exclusively in this medium. Most judges do not and cannot know the inner workings of the business that are so necessary and helpful in making a fair determination of a theatrical dispute.

3. Arbitration may be less expensive. Since arbitration dispenses with formal court procedures, it may take considerably less time, and would thus save substantial money.

4. Arbitration may result in a more equitable solution. Where the emphasis is on content rather than form, it may be easier to accomplish the correct result. At the risk of antagonizing some law-

yers and some judges, it must be noted that the rules of evidence which have governed our court procedure for hundreds of years may force the judge to make a decision without the benefit of facts which an arbitrator would have access to because of the streamlined arbitration procedures.

Bear in mind that the specific terms of each of the previously enumerated items will be different in each union-approved contract.

The differences are not between the agreement used by one agent and the agreement used by another. All franchised agents use the same union-approved contract. The differences are between the provisions in one union contract and another union contract. The SAG agency agreement differs from the AFTRA agency agreement, which differs from the AGVA agency agreement, and so on.

For an example, the period of time that the actor must be unemployed before the contract may be cancelled varies from contract to contract. What constitutes unemployment will be different in each contract. In one instance, the actor must be employed in the field covered by the contract, and in another instance, in any field in the entertainment industry during a specified period of time to preclude a contract's termination due to lack of employment.

The rest of the fine print in those big, long contracts consists of refinements, fine distinctions, definitions, and additional incidental terms.

But these are the basics you should be aware of and should know are part of each contract you sign.

For our purposes, we will analyze the Actors Equity agency agreement and the AFTRA agency agreement in some detail and will thereafter make a cursory reference to the other agreements without going into a detailed analysis of the specific provisions.

It isn't that the Equity and AFTRA agreements are more important than the others; it's just that this seemed the expedient thing to do. At the time this is being written, all of the standard employment agreements of AFTRA (not the Agency Representation Agreement) are being renegotiated. For this reason, the standard SAG employment agreements (rather than the AFTRA employment agreements) are discussed in greater detail and the SAG agency agreement receives less detailed attention while the AFTRA agency agreement gets detailed consideration.

In discussing the SAG agency agreement, we will see, for example, that it may be terminated if a certain amount of work is not offered during a certain period of time; however, rather than define this amount of work, we will simply call attention to the existence of the provision. Under discussion of the Equity and AFTRA agency agreements, these provisions are discussed in detail to give you the basic understanding of the terms.

Quite a few of the agency contracts have a specific reference that is applicable to California only. A certain section of the California law regulates the relationship of members of a labor union with employment agencies. Accordingly, the contracts (in some instances as part of the contract, and in other instances as part of a rider) make reference to the specific section of the California Labor

Code, and also note that the Labor Commissioner of the State of California must be notified of the time and place of any arbitration proceding, and that the Commissioner or his authorized representative has the right to attend the arbitration. This provision appears, either as a rider or as part of the contract, in the Actors Equity contract, the AFTRA contract, both SAG contracts, the AFM Exclusive Agent Musician Agreement, the AGVA contract, a general services contract in use and in certain of the other miscellaneous catchall contracts covering items not dealt with in the union-approved agreements.

The performer in the various agency agreements is referred to as the "actor," as the "artist," as the "musician," and sometimes even as the "performer," and will be similarly referred to in this book.

The agency may be referred to in the agreements and in this book as the "agent" or "manager."

All this adds up to the fact that we should make careful distinctions between the various kinds of representatives. An actor or writer may be represented by an agent, a manager, an attorney, his mother, or his friend. One who acts for another will be referred to as a representative, of which there are various kinds.

There are also several kinds of agents, and this gets very confusing. There are talent agents and there are literary agents. Since talent agents represent actors and seek to find employment for them, they must be licensed and union-approved, as we discussed. Literary agents, on the other hand, need not be licensed, because they are selling a property rather than finding work for the client.

If this isn't confusing enough, just consider the types of managers. There are "personal managers" and "exclusive managers." Neither need be licensed, but exclusive managers, as will be seen later in greater detail, must be approved by the musicians unions, the AFM and AGMA. And, as we will see, although managers may not find employment, since they are not licensed, an exclusive manager may find an engagement for his opera or ballet star who would not be an "employee" but an "independent contractor." But more of this later.

An attorney—oh well, everyone knows what he does or is supposed to do.

AGENCY

AGREEMENTS

AGENCY AGREEMENT
ACTORS' EQUITY ASSOCIATION

Actors Equity Association has codified the rules and regulations which affect the actor-agent relationship. The exclusive management contract which is a standard form (that is, it is the same form used by all agents) is governed by a set of rules published by Equity known as "Rule A." In fact, the exclusive management contract which each actor signs specifically states that it incorporates in it the provisions of Rule A.

Your agent is obligated to do certain things for you. It isn't just a case that he "ought to," but rather, there is a contractual obligation binding him to do so. The hooker in the deal is that although the agent is legally, contractually obligated, it is next to impossible to prove a breach of most of the obligations, because of the difficulty, or the impossibility, of proving such a breach. For example, the agent must:

1. Counsel and advise the actor when asked to do so.
2. Be truthful and not conceal pertinent facts.
3. Use reasonable efforts to assist the actor to procure acting work.

4. Consider only the actor's interest in representing him.
5. Read scripts in which the actor is interested.
6. Seek out and speak with producers.
7. Continue to be equipped to represent the actor ably and diligently in the legitimate theatre industry.

The catch: how does one effectively convince an arbitrator that his agent has not counseled or advised him, or that he has not used reasonable efforts to find work for him, or that he has not read a script in which the actor has an interest?

There are other requirements. For example, the agent must:

1. Make no binding commitment without the actor's approval and without informing the actor of the terms.
2. Be available at reasonable times to represent the actor, negotiate, and attend conferences.
3. Give business advice and perform in a competent manner.

Again, how does one convince an arbitrator that the agent was not performing in a competent manner? Some things could perhaps be proven, but only with great difficulty.

Strangely enough, however, Rule A contains a provision that is not in the contract, and the contract contains a provision that is not in Rule A. The contract provision is to the effect that before the contract is entered into, if the actor requests, the agent must deliver a list of the actors of the same qualifications as the actor, persons who would be eligible for the same parts or roles, who are represented by the agent. Of course the agent is permitted to represent such people, but if the actor wants to know who would be specifically competing with him, he may find out.

The provision in Rule A not included in the contract provides that the actor may request in writing (but not more often than once every four weeks) detailed written information setting forth what efforts the agent has rendered on his behalf. This is in accord with the idea that an actor ought to know at least what his agent has or has not been doing on his behalf.

Under rare circumstances one might prove that an agent's conflict of interest interfered with proper representation of the actor, or that the agent engaged in dishonest or fraudulent activity. But, let's face it, the contract is binding and not easy for an actor to get out of (unless there has been no theatre work, as later noted) and the assumption has to be that an agent will knock his brains out, or at least try to, for a given actor, not because the contract says he has to—or else, but rather because it is to the agent's interest for the actor to do well and make lots of money.

If an actor fails to be employed or does not receive payment for two weeks' work in the legitimate theatre at his usual salary during any period of 120 days, then either the actor or the agent may terminate the contract by giving the other party written notice. However, the right to so terminate is subject to the following qualifications:

The 120-day period is extended:

1. During any period that the actor says he is unavailable.

2. During any time the actor is physically or men-
tally unable to work.

3. During such time that the actor is unavailable and
employed in a field outside the legitimate theatre
industry.

If we analyze this carefully we can see that there are
difficulties which may confront most actors who would like
to terminate an agency contract. First, it should be noted
that the clause is carefully worded to read ". . . fails to be
employed . . . in the legitimate theatre industry." There is
no requirement that the agent must have found the two
weeks' employment, assisted in negotiating the terms, or
even, for that matter, knew that the job was available.

Most actors are not rich enough that they can remain
unemployed for very much longer than 120 days. The fre-
quent complaint of many an actor who would like to use
this clause to terminate the contract is that he worked
because he had to, and that he found the job himself. If
the job was for at least two weeks in theatre, then a new
120-day period starts from the time of termination of the
job, and if it were any kind of work other than theatre, and
the actor is unavailable for a theatre job, the 120-day
period is extended accordingly. As sometimes (maybe
often) happens, an actor will find work himself in spite of
the agent, and in so doing extends the length of time of
the agent's contract with him.

There is still another "out" for the agent. If before the

expiration of the 120 days the actor is under contract to work during the 120 days following the 120 days of insufficient employment, and he works at least six weeks at his usual salary, which six weeks' employment may occur in both 120-day periods combined (during the 240 days), then the actor may not terminate the contract. Again, there is no requirement that the six weeks' work need be a result of the agent's efforts, that the agent negotiate the employment contracts, or that the agent even know of the employment.

If an agent does absolutely nothing for his client and the client is industrious enough and lucky enough, the actor may create the very employment which prevents his leaving his agent who has done nothing for him.

The period of employment guaranteed by the contract is satisfied to the extent that the actor finds work at his usual salary, at or near the actor's usual place of employment, in computing the time worked to determine whether the actor may terminate the contract.

The agency contract is usually entered into for a period of three years, and it may not be for more than three years. If this is the first exclusive management contract between the actor and the agent, then the contract may not be for a period longer than one year, unless a certain set of circumstances exists. If the actor has had a written agency contract with the agent in other parts of the entertainment industry which has been in effect for at least a year, then this initial contract may be for more than a year, but no longer than the remaining term of the contract between the actor and agent in the other part of the entertainment industry. If there is more than one contract, the term may be as long as the longest remaining term, but in no event more than three years.

The agent's commission under this agreement is not the usual 10% as is often believed. It may not be more than 10%, and under certain circumstances it will be less.

If the actor receives less than $1,000 per week, then the commission is 5% of the first $200 each week, and 10% of the balance over the $200 during any such week.

If the actor receives less than $50 more than the Equity Production Minimum or Industrial Show Minimum, then the agent may not receive more than 5% for a maximum of the first ten weeks of each employment contract.

On stock engagements, the agent may receive up to 10% of the actor's earnings; however, if the actor receives less than $1,000 per week, then the agent may only be paid 5% of the first $300 and only for a maximum of the first ten weeks.

AGENCY AGREEMENT

AMERICAN FEDERATION OF TELEVISION AND RADIO ARTISTS

As the name implies, this is a standard contract engaging the agent to represent the artist in the transcription, radio broadcasting, and television industries as is set forth in AFTRA's Rule 12B. This seems simple enough, however there may be some question as to whether or not the AFTRA regulations or the SAG regulations cover a particular employment in the television industry. For example, there is some confusion with respect to T.V. commercials, which will be discussed later in greater detail.

AFTRA's Rule 12B states that "television," "television broadcasting industry," and "television broadcasting field" mean the television field within AFTRA's jurisdiction. Under the SAG Television Motion Picture Artists–Manager Contract which we will discuss later, the contract provides that it is applicable to television motion pictures as defined in the SAG Regulations Amended Rule 16F.

The agency contract may also cover the artist's (the actor is referred to as the "artist" in this agreement) services in recording for phonograph records, provided that a specific rider is annexed to the standard contract and initialed by the artist.

In the agreement, the artist agrees that he will become a member of AFTRA if he is not a member before he takes on an engagement under AFTRA's jurisdiction. Of course, the artist warrants, that is, he states and guarantees that he is not represented by any other agent, since this is an exclusive agency contract. The agent, on the other hand, warrants or agrees that he will remain a duly franchised agent of AFTRA. The term of the contract is set forth, not to be in excess of three years.

The artist agrees to pay the agent a sum not in excess of 10% of the monies which the artist receives under contracts of employment during the term of the contract. The money is payable only when it is received by the artist or someone on the artist's behalf, which of course would mean when received by the agent.

The agent is also entitled to 10% of any sums received on settlement or termination of a contract; however, the actor may first deduct any arbitration fees, attorney's fees, or court costs before computing the amount. Compensation is also paid on employment contracts entered into during the agency contract term which may extend past the term of the agency contract.

The AFTRA agency contract is somewhat unusual in that it provides that the minimum scale set forth for actors is the minimum which they must be paid after deduction of the agency commission. This means that unless the actor is paid more than the AFTRA minimum scale, the agent will not receive a commission.

What sometimes happens is that in the negotiations for a job, the actor's agent may insist that the actor be paid by the producer an amount referred to as "scale plus." Scale, of course, means the minimum union-approved amount and the "plus" is the amount of the agent's commission computed on the minimum amount. In this way the agent would make certain that the actor is paid enough by the producer to cover the actor's fee and the agent's fee.

The actor may not terminate an employment contract and enter into a similar contract with the same employer within 60 days of the agency contract termination, or the agent must be paid his percentage on such an engagement. Each day between June 15th and September 16th is counted as 3/5 of a day in figuring the 60 days. The agent is not entitled to any percentage on the increase in payments in the new employment contract if the agency contract is not then in effect.

The agent agrees that he will be of service to the actor as long as he receives commissions. The agent's commissions are computed on gross receipts without deduction for Social Security, old age pension, or other tax payments.

If the agent conveys a job offer to the actor in writing, and the actor accepts such employment within 90 days thereafter, then the agent is entitled to a commission on such employment even if the term of the agency contract has expired.

There is a provision in this agreement similar to the Equity agreement provision to the effect that the contract may be terminated if the actor is not employed for a certain length of time during a certain period. There are, of course, some differences in the Equity and AFTRA agreements. In the AFTRA agreement it is provided that either party, that is, the agent or the actor, may terminate the agency contract on notice in writing if during any 91 days the actor fails to be employed or entitled to receive payment for 15 days in any branch of the entertainment industry either under AFTRA's jurisdiction or otherwise.

For the purposes of computing the 15 days' employment, each separate original radio broadcast, whether live or recorded, and each transcribed program, is considered a day's employment; however, a rebroadcast, whether recorded or live, or an off-the-line recording, or a prior recording, or time spent in rehearsal, is not considered employment. During the months of June, July, and August, each day's employment is considered 1-1/2 days'

| 41

employment for the purposes of this computation. Each separate television broadcast (including the rehearsal time) is considered 2-1/2 days' employment. However, more than 3 days spent in rehearsal, inclusive of the day of the telecast, and any days of exclusivity over 3 days inclusive of the day of telecast, automatically extends the 91 day period by such overage. During the months of June, July, and August, each day's employment in the television broadcasting field for the purpose of computing the 15 days is considered 3-3/4 days' employment. A master phonograph record is considered one day's employment.

As with the Equity contract, if the agent gives the artist notice in writing of a job offer at the artist's usual place of employment at a salary commensurate with the artist's prestige, then the artist must take the employment or the proposed employment time guaranteed will be considered time worked or compensation received by the artist in computing the time worked or money earned in determining the artist's right to terminate the contract.

Termination of the contract by the artist will not deprive the agent of commissions which he is otherwise entitled to.

The artist also may not terminate the contract if at the time he attempts to do so any one of the following circumstances exists:

1. The artist is working under a contract which guarantees employment in the broadcasting industry for at least one program each week for a period of not less than 13 consecutive weeks. A program is

considered either a regional network program of one-half hour length or more, or a national network program of one-quarter hour length or more, or a program or programs the aggregate weekly compensation for which equals or exceeds the artist's customary compensation for either a one-half hour regional network program or a one-quarter hour national network program.

2. If the artist is actually working under a written contract or contracts which guarantee the artist either employment in the television broadcasting field for at least one program every other week in a cycle of 13 consecutive weeks where the program is telecast on an alternate week basis, or employment for at least 8 programs in a cycle of 39 consecutive weeks, where the program is telecast on a monthly basis or is telecast once every four weeks.

3. The artist is under written contract as described above in paragraphs (1) and (2) and such contract begins within 45 days after the time the artist attempts to terminate the contract.

4. If the artist attempts to terminate the contract during the months of August or September, and the artist is under a written contract as described in paragraphs (1) and (2) above, and such contract begins not later than October 15th.

5. If during the period of 91 days immediately preceding the giving of notice of termination the artist has received or has been entitled to receive compensation in an amount equal to not less than

13 times his past customary compensation for a national network program of one-half hour length whether the employment is from the broadcasting industries or any other branch of the entertainment industry in which the agent is authorized to act for the artist.

The artist also may not terminate the contract if he is under contract in the entertainment industry in any field in which the agent is authorized to act for him where, during the succeeding period of 182 days after the expiration of the 91-day period, the artist is entitled to a guaranteed compensation of $25,000 or more, or where the artist is under a contract or contracts for the rendition of services during such 182-day period in the radio, phonograph recording, and/or television fields at a guaranteed compensation of $20,000 or more.

Periods of lay-off or leaves of absence under a "term contract" are not deemed periods of unemployment unless the contract provides that the artist has the right during such period to do other work in the radio or television field or any other branch of the entertainment industry in which the agent represents him. A "term contract" means a contract in which the artist is guaranteed employment in the broadcasting industries for at least one program each week for a period of not less than 13 consecutive weeks or at least one program every other week in a cycle of 13 weeks, where a program is telecast on an alternate week basis. It also includes a contract providing employment for at least 8 programs in a cycle of 39 consecutive weeks, where the program is telecast monthly or is telecast every four weeks. A term contract is defined in the regulations of the Screen Actors Guild, Inc. with respect to the motion picture industry is also considered a term contract for this purpose.

There are provisions in the agreement covering a situation where a contract of employment is cancelled. Bear in mind that if the artist is paid, even though he does not perform in a broadcast for which he has been employed, this is nevertheless considered employment. The 91-day period is also extended in the event that broadcasting over a majority of both the radio stations as well as a majority of the television broadcasting stations is suspended, which would cover a situation where there is a strike or other similar calamity which would suspend broadcasting for some period of time. Of course, the agent may represent other persons in the business and need not devote his entire time and attention to the business of one artist.

The agency agreement, like the Actors Equity Agreement, sets forth the names of not more than four persons in the agency who will be available to the artist and with whom he can communicate. One of these persons is required to be available at all reasonable times for consultation with the artist for the purpose of negotiating contracts.

There is also provision for setting forth not more than four names of agents, and if three or four persons are named, at least two of these persons must remain active in the agency during the term of the contract. In the event that only one or two persons are named in the contract, then at least one of the persons named must remain active in the agency. This provision is to insure that the artist is represented by someone with whom the artist has rapport and in whom the artist has confidence. As in the Actors Equity contract, the agent agrees that he:

1. Will not enter into any contracts for the artist at less than the AFTRA minimum.
2. Will counsel and advise the artist in connection with his professional matters.
3. Will be truthful with the artist.
4. Will not bind the artist without the artist's approval.
5. Is a fiduciary.

The fact that the agent is a fiduciary has important legal significance. This means that he acts on behalf of the principal (the artist), for the principal, and that there are strict legal requirements that a fiduciary exercise a certain measure of care in attending to the artist's business, and in caring for any of the artist's money which may come into his hands.

The agent asserts that he is equipped and will continue to be equipped to represent the artist and that he will do so diligently. He says that he will use all reasonable efforts to assist the artist in procuring employment in the broadcasting industries. The agent states that he will maintain an office and telephone which is open during all reasonable business hours within the city of New York (or such other city where he has an office) or its environs and that he will be present at the office during such business hours.

The artist may request, not more often than once every four weeks, that the agent give him information in writing stating what efforts the agent has rendered on his behalf.

There is also provision that the agent will not charge or collect any commissions on compensation received by the artist for services rendered by the artist in a package show in which the agent is interested, where prohibited by the AFTRA regulations. This is to avoid the agent's collecting commissions under circumstances where he represents the employer of the artist and thus be involved in a conflict of interest. The rules define what it means for an agent to be interested in a package show or engaged in package show activities.

The contract provides that the AFTRA regulations govern the interpretation of the contract, and that in the event of a dispute, the matter is to be submitted to arbitration.

The AFTRA contract may have a rider attached to it which provides that the agency contract may be extended for a certain period under certain circumstances; however, the extended period, together with the original term, cannot exceed three years. Thus, it is possible for the original agency contract to be for a period of one year and to provide for two additional extended terms of one year each.

There's also a possibility of a rider being annexed which provides that the artist will pay the agent commissions on contracts of employment in existence at the time the contract is entered into with the agent; however, this would not be applicable if the artist is already obligated to pay a commission to another agent on such existing employment contracts.

AGENCY AGREEMENT

SCREEN ACTORS GUILD, INC.

There are two SAG agency contracts, one covering television motion pictures and the other covering theatrical motion pictures. SAG (not just AFTRA) has jurisdiction over many of the television commercials, those which are considered to be television motion pictures, and others, in many instances even where they are not, in fact, on film. This joint jurisdiction of commercials, and the division between the unions, is discussed in detail later in connection with the SAG standard employment contracts (as distinguished from the standard agency contracts here discussed) .

In any event, the agent may represent the actor for motion picture commercials (or other SAG commercials even if not actually in fact made on film) only if the actor has initialed (with the exception later noted where initialing is not necessary) a part of the SAG Agency Television Motion Picture Contract granting the agent this authority.

If the actor enters into a series or term employment contract for services in a television motion picture in which he also agrees to render services in program commercials or spots, or enters into a free-lance contract for services in a single television motion picture and agrees to render services in program commercials for use only with this television motion picture, then the agency contract includes representation of the actor in connection with his employment in such commercials, whether or not the agency contract is specifically initialed to grant the agent this authority.

Just as the two SAG contracts have much in common with the Equity, AFTRA, and AGVA contracts, they have even more in common with each other, in that about half of each SAG agreement uses the identical language.

The television motion picture contract provides that the actor employs the agent for television motion pictures as defined in the applicable SAG rules, and the theatrical motion picture contract has a similar provision with respect to theatrical motion pictures.

Both SAG agency contracts set forth the length of the term, and both provide that the agent will be paid 10% of the monies received. There is a discussion of agency commissions on domestic reruns in the television motion picture contract, and a discussion of the fact that certain payments for travel or living expenses are excluded in computing the agent's commissions in theatrical motion picture agreements.

Both contracts have general language setting forth how the agency commission is computed. As in the other approved agency contracts, if employment commences during the agency contract period and continues after the term of the contract, then the agent is also entitled to commissions on the work done after the contract expires.

Similar to the other agency contracts, there is a provision in both SAG contracts to the effect that an actor may not terminate an employment contract and enter into a similar contract with the same employer within 60 days after the end of the agency's representation. This would be a means of avoiding a payment of a justly earned agency commission and would not be permissible. The agent's commissions are payable only on monies actually received.

Both SAG contracts have a provision to the effect that if the actor is not employed during a specified period (which happens in both instances to be 91 days), then the contract may be terminated under certain specified conditions. The method of computing the 91 days is discussed in detail in each of the agreements, and those circumstances which would prevent the actor from terminating the contract are set forth.

As in the other approved agency contracts, the SAG contracts provide that one person at the agency must be available at all reasonable times for consultation with the actor, and that the agent will maintain telephone service in the office. In the event of a controversy there is a provision for arbitration.

AGENCY AGREEMENT
AMERICAN GUILD OF VARIETY ARTISTS

Like the Equity, AFTRA and SAG agency contracts, the

AGVA agency contract provides that the agent will exclusively represent the artist in employment under the jurisdiction of this union which of course covers vaudeville and the variety entertainment field.

As with the other contracts, the artist agrees that he will join the union and remain a member in good standing.

The term of the contract may not be for more than three years; however, this contract may be extended for a further term of not more than an additional three years if certain things occur as set forth in the agreement. If the contract is for 180 days or less, the agent must give notice not later than the beginning of the last third of the term if he wishes to extend it; and if the artist wishes to terminate it, under such circumstances he must also give notice so as to permit the parties to arbitrate the extension in the event of a dispute.

The agent is entitled to receive not in excess of 10% of the gross receipts earned by the artist from jobs under AGVA jurisdiction, and the payment is made as with the other contracts, when received by the artist or by someone on his behalf. Any jobs which continue after the termination of the agency contract are jobs for which the agent is entitled to receive compensation. As with the other agreements, before computing the amount due the agent, arbitration fees, reasonable attorney's fees, reasonable expenses, and court costs if they are due are first deducted.

The artist cannot have a contract of substitution within a 90-day period after the termination of the agency contract, which means that he cannot within the 90 days enter into the same contract which was terminated while he was still represented by the agent. This would be an obvious means of avoiding the payment due to the agent.

As in the other agency agreements, there is provision that the artist may terminate the contract if during any period of 90 days he is not employed in any field under AGVA jurisdiction, or in any other branch of the entertainment industry in which the agent represents the artist. There are specific qualifications of this provision set forth in detail in the agreement.

The artist asserts in the agreement that he is a certain age, and grants the agent the right to use his name and photograph to advertise and publicize him. The agent agrees:

1. To abide by the minimums established by AGVA.
2. To inform the artist and to counsel and advise him in matters concerning him in the variety field.
3. To be truthful in his statements to the artist.
4. To make no binding agreements or commitments on behalf of the artist without the approval of the artist or without first informing him of the terms and conditions.
5. To act as a fiduciary.
6. Not to disclose information with reference to the artist's affairs.

The agent states that:

1. He is equipped and will continue to be equipped to represent the artist.
2. He will represent him in the variety field.

3. He will use his best efforts to procure or assist the artist in procuring employment.

The contract also contains the California clause previously mentioned, which provides that the Labor Commissioner of the State of California will be given notice of any arbitrations, and that he will have the right to attend all arbitration hearings.

AGENCY AGREEMENT

AMERICAN GUILD OF MUSICAL ARTISTS

The American Guild of Musical Artists has a standard artist's management contract which a performer signs to engage a representative. You will note that I used the word "representative" rather than "agent" for, in fact, a person in the concert, recital, oratorio, opera, and ballet fields in the U. S. and Canada may be represented by a licensed agent or by an unlicensed manager. The performer's representative, in this area, is generally referred to as an "exclusive manager."

An exclusive manager need not be a licensed agent to work for an opera or ballet performer, for the manager is not really seeking "employment," but rather, is seeking an "engagement." This might seem a fine distinction, but it is legally an important one, and because of this important legal difference, an exclusive manager need not be licensed.

| 53

For example, an opera star is hired in a different manner than a dramatic actor, and the nature of the employment is different. An opera star falls into the legal classification of an "independent contractor." An independent contractor performs whatever he wishes, has his own accompanist, rehearses as he wishes, and is not subject to the producer's direction. He is, in effect, his own boss and not an employee. A similar example in everyday life would be the case of a plumber you might hire to fix your sink. He would be an independent contractor. You would instruct him what sink to fix, but he would do it in his own fashion. He would not be considered an employee of yours. Of course, there are other distinctions between an independent contractor and an employee. An independent contractor is paid a fee without any deductions for social security or tax withheld. Indeed, you know that an employee ends up with a weekly paycheck considerably less than what he is paid because of these deductions.

Thus, opera stars are represented by managers, some of whom are licensed agents, and some of whom are not. An actor works for the producer. The opera star works for himself.

The standard artist's manager contract, in addition to setting forth the fact that the manager is an exclusive manager, will also set forth the term of the contract and the fact that it may be extended for additional terms. Since each artist is an independent contractor, the artist's fees for certain kinds of work will vary.

There are fixed minimums in the field of opera, but not in the concert field. There is a schedule of minimums for operatic performers. Each role in each opera has a different minimum, and these minimums vary from opera company to opera company. I am informed that the Metropolitan Opera in New York is an exception in that the roles are not classified in this fashion. It seems a staggering job to anticipate fixing a different minimum for each role in each opera, in each company, and I am sure whenever these minimum fees are renegotiated, it is an overwhelming chore.

Each artist, of course, has an idea as to what his own particular minimum fee is for different kinds of work. The Standard Artists' Management Contract has three blanks to be filled in which set forth minimums for the performer, and by which the manager is bound. The performer's minimum fees as set forth may be considerably greater than the Guild's minimum fees fixed for a particular role. The management contract, when filled in, will state that the artist will be paid different minimums per engagement for the following kinds of engagements:

Regular concerts;

Symphony orchestra engagements; and

Civic, community, and similarly organized concert engagements.

The manager's fee is also set forth and he may not charge more than 20% on regular concert engagements, not more than 15% on civic, community and similarly organized concert engagements, and not more than 10% on operatic and ballet engagements.

The manager agrees to use his best efforts for the artist and to turn over the artist's money to him. The artist agrees to conscientiously fulfill the engagements, to notify the manager of all inquiries, and to be responsible for all traveling and promotional expenses.

Each manager who represents artists under this management contract must sign a basic agreement with AGMA and must agree to be bound by the agreement and the AGMA rules. This is similar, in effect, to being franchised, in that it constitutes recognition by the union that this particular representative may act on behalf of the union's members, and in so acting will act within certain defined limits.

AGENCY AGREEMENT

AMERICAN FEDERATION OF MUSICIANS

A musician may engage an agent for a term not in excess of five years. The agent is employed as the musician's exclusive agent and manager throughout the world with respect to the musician's services, appearances, and endeavors as a musician. It should be noted that the representation by the agent covers not only the musician who signs with the agent, but also all musicians who perform with any orchestra or group led or conducted by the signing musician, whom the signing musician makes subject to the terms of the agency agreement.

The agent agrees:

1. To assist the musician to obtain offers of work.

2. To negotiate engagements for the musician.

3. To advise, aid, counsel, and guide the musician with respect to his professional career.

4. To promote and advertise the musician's name and talents.

5. To carry on correspondence in his behalf.

6. To cooperate with other representatives of the musician to perform these duties.

As with the other agency agreements, the agent agrees to maintain an office, staff and facilities adequate for the performance of his duties and agrees that he will not accept any engagements for the musician without the musician's prior approval. The musician must, however, agree that he will not unreasonably withhold approval for any engagements.

The agent can perform other, similar services for other musicians and may engage in other businesses and ventures. The musician is obligated to refer all job communications to the agent. The agency agreement is for exclusive employment, and the musician may not employ another agent, but can, of course, employ a personal manager. The agent can publicize the fact that he represents the musician and may authorize others to use the musician's name and photograph for publicity.

The contract has a provision that if the musician breaches the agreement, the only remedy to which the agent is entitled is to receive commissions on monies received by the musician.

The agent is entitled to receive 10% if the musician is

engaged in excess of three days, plus an additional 5% if the net monies or other consideration received for the engagement equals or exceeds twice the applicable minimum scale of the AFM or any AFM local union having jurisdiction over the engagement. If the engagement is for three days or less, then the agent is entitled to receive 20%. In no event may the musician receive less than the applicable minimum scale of the AFM or any AFM local having jurisdiction over the job.

The agent cannot receive a commission in excess of the amount in the agreement, and if the agent receives a commission, fee, or other consideration from any other source for supplying the services of the musician, he must report it to the musician and deduct the amount from the commission payable by the musician. The commission is due when and if the money is received.

The musician may initial a part of the contract which permits the agent to take a commission on engagements in existence at the time the contract is entered into on condition that the musician is not under any obligation to pay commissions to another agent for the same engagement. The monies commissionable are, as in other agreements, defined, and there are certain deductions from the gross receipts permitted in the computation. In the case of musicians, however, in addition to some of the usual deductions allowed in other contracts, such as expenses incurred in collecting funds, including the costs of arbitration, litigation, and attorney's fees, musicians are also permitted to deduct transportation costs, dues, dues equivalents, fees, and other monies payable to the AFM, or any local of the AFM, in determining the amount of money which is commissionable.

There is provision in the agreement for the musician to advance part of the agent's commission to him if the musician wishes to do so and if that specific provision is initialed by the musician.

The agreement is for five years, but may be automatically extended for an additional two years, unless the musician does not obtain a certain minimal amount of employment as set forth in the agreement.

There is also provision for termination by either the agent or the musician under certain specific circumstances set forth.

All controversies must be determined by the International Board of the AFM in accordance with the rules of the Board. However, the standard clause referring to the State of California is included which provides that the Labor Commissioner must receive notice of and may attend any arbitration.

Both parties agree that they will not enter into negotiations or agree to a renewal or extension of the agreement before the beginning of the final two years of the original term of the agreement.

AGENCY REPRESENTATIVES

With the various standard agency contracts in use, one must wonder how these contracts came into existence and who negotiates the contracts for the agencies, since each agency uses an identical agreement for each union. The logical conclusion would be that the agencies have their own association to negotiate for them, just as Broadway producers and theatre owners negotiate through the League of New York Theatres.

If it makes sense that the agents should have an association, does it make more or less sense that they should have two or more associations, as they do? It might help to understand why this happened to know that an agent might have more in common with certain agents who operate in his particular field than with others who operate largely in different fields. A big agency, with its diverse clients' interests, would be likely to have something in common with all agents. Bearing this in mind, one might better understand why the agencies have at least three associations to represent them in different areas of negotiation.

The ARA (Artists Representatives Association Inc.) negotiates with AFTRA on behalf of the agents. As a matter of fact, ARA, which is on the East Coast, negotiates jointly with AMG (Artists Managers Guild), a West Coast association, in representing the agents in the AFTRA and SAG negotiations. It seems that ARA takes the lead in AFTRA negotiations and AMG probably takes the lead in the SAG negotiations. This might have resulted from the fact that the film industry was and still is located largely on the West Coast, and television, on the other hand, was East Coast-centered. ARA also seems to take the lead in negotiations with AGVA.

The Actors Equity Association contract negotiations with agents are handled by TARA (Theatrical Artists

Representatives Association). One should also bear in mind that there is a Society of Authors' Representatives which negotiates on behalf of literary agents, and other, less formal groups, which get together from time to time, such as an organization of agents dealing largely in the area of commercials.

Some of these groups do more than just represent agents in negotiations. For example, ARA collects the annual franchise fee from all of the AFTRA-franchised agents, and forwards a check in one lump sum to AFTRA.

AGENCY CATCHALL CONTRACTS

As noted in the introduction to this book, there are a group of contracts which some agents use which I will refer to as "catchall contracts." Unlike the standard contracts approved by the unions, these agreements are not standard; that is, there is no one particular contract used by all agencies. There may be similarities between some of the various contracts used by different agencies, but they are generally different contracts attempting to accomplish the same purpose: namely, to commit the actor or writer to representation in as many areas as possible for as long a time as possible. The contracts generally are called different things by different agencies, even when drafted in such a manner as to cover the same items and to accomplish the same result.

It goes without saying that a catchall contract may not be applicable to anything covered by a standard union-approved contract. Since many catchalls are written so broadly as to include anything and everything, some do state in them that any employment covered by a union-approved agreement is excluded from the coverage of the contract.

AGENCY GENERAL SERVICES CONTRACTS

Your agent, when he signs you, may present you with a document with the label "General Services" or some other similar name which is intended to cover his representation of you in all branches of the entertainment, publication, and related industries throughout the world, including merchandising, testimonials, and other business involvements. Such a contract has the usual clauses stating that the agent will promote and advance your professional career, and that he will be rendering similar services to others.

This kind of agreement usually provides that he will be paid a commission of 10% of the gross compensation which you or any person, firm, or corporation on your behalf, directly, or indirectly, receives for your services. (There may be a good tax reason for a corporation owned by you to be paid for your services. The corporation would of course pay you a salary as its employee.) It may also provide that the agent is entitled to 15% of any sums received by you for lectures, concerts, readings, recitals, and any other engagements presented in places where concerts, lectures, readings, and recitals are given, as well as tours constituting, or similar to, concerts, lectures, readings, and recitals. The contract covers all extensions, renewals, or substitutions for any such engagements and may define a substitution either as a contract resumed within three, four, or five months immediately after the previous engagement.

If you receive any proceeds from a motion picture, film, tape, wire, transcription, recording, or other reproduction, then the agent is entitled to receive commissions as long as any of these are used, sold, leased, or otherwise disposed of, whether during or after the term of the contract. This is particularly bothersome, since the contract provides for payment to the agent on agreements already in existence at the time the agent is signed. The language of the contract would seem to entitle the agent to commissions on the listed items forever; however, it may be argued that this surely is not what is intended by the agreement, even though it specifically seems to say this.

This kind of language is particularly vague and all-inclusive. The contract ought to delineate more clearly the areas of representation and the time of the representation, unless the agent intends to represent you for all time, in all of these areas of endeavor. Such may be the case and such may be his intention.

In the event that you are employed by a corporation in which you are one of the owners, then the corporation also is obligated to payment of commissions for your services.

The agent must be notified of, and given an opportunity to remedy any claimed breach of the agreement.

Included is a provision that applies within the jurisdicdiction of the Labor Commissioner of California, to the effect that either party under certain circumstances may terminate the agreement if the actor does not have any employment or a bona fide offer for the disposition of any material for four months or more.

AGENCY GENERAL MATERIALS AND PACKAGES CONTRACTS

Most agents have a form which covers general materials and packages, in which you appoint the agent as your sole and exclusive representative anywhere in the world to deal with all creative properties and package shows controlled, acquired, or created in whole or in part by you or any firm or corporation owned or controlled by you. This kind of agreement contains many provisions similar to those in the general services contract just discussed.

There may be a provision that the agent can represent other clients of his in negotiations with you. In such event he would not be representing you, so you would have to find other representation or go it alone, which is not a recommended procedure.

The contract specifically covers creative packages and includes syndication, merchandising, advertising, testimonials, and business involvements, as well as stock and amateur stage rights in and to the creative properties or package shows.

You will pay 10% of your gross compensation to the agent for creative properties or package shows, 15% for printed publication in the British Empire, and 20% for printed publication in other countries. The agreement may also provide that you pay 15% for concerts, lectures, readings, and appearances of a similar nature, including engagements and tours for dramatic or musical shows. It will probably provide that you will pay 20% for receipts from amateur stage performances of your properties. If a correspondent agent is required outside the United States, you may be required to pay an additional 5% to the correspondent agent.

In computing "gross compensation" the agent must deduct from the total receipts any amounts actually paid to a third party who syndicates reproductions and is entitled to a distribution fee, as well as print costs and advertising costs if actually paid to or retained by the distributor.

One agency uses an agreement which defines a creative property to include anything you might imagine. The definition lists rights, interests, properties, and material of a literary, entertainment, advertising, and promotion nature, including:

art	characters	characterizations
compositions	copyrights	designs
dramatic and/or		
musical works	drawings	formats
formulas	ideas	outlines
literary works	music	lyrics
musical		
arrangements	bits of business	actions
incidents	plots	treatments
scripts	sketches	themes (literary
titles	names	and musical)
trade names	patents	trademarks
catchwords	writings	slogans

or any part or combination of any of the foregoing or any other rights, interests, properties, or materials which may be acquired, written, composed, or utilized for or in connection therewith, including any creative property or package show based upon or produced as part of, or developed from, any element of any creative property or package show covered by this agreement. Whew! Could they possibly have overlooked anything? That seems to cover just about everything, now doesn't it?

A definition of package shows is just about as detailed.

This contract also requires payment to the agent on agreements in existence at the time the agent is signed, even though he may have had nothing to do with the agreement.

AGENCY CREATIVE PROPERTY AND
PACKAGE PROGRAM CONTRACTS

Another agency having a packages representation agreement defines "creative property and package program" similarly as any and all literary, artistic, entertainment, educational or commercial creations and materials, and all rights, properties, and material resulting—including:

literary, dramatic, and musical material

ideas	themes	plots
slogans	designs	copyrights
characters	titles	trade names
trademarks	books	plays
dramas	stories	episodes

recordings	scripts	motion pictures
shows	package, radio, and television
musical	programs	
compositions	musical	choreographic
	orchestrations	works

and artistic compositions of any kind as well as any other creative properties or package programs which use the title, basic idea, basic format, basic characters, basic characterizations, or any artistic or creative element of, or literary material contained in, any of the foregoing. This agency agreement has the other provisions similar to the one just discussed. It provides that 10% of the gross monies received are payable to the agent for any sales made. Sales agreements covering the concert field and amateur stage performances call for payment of 20% of the gross receipts.

What appears to be somewhat puzzling is that the contract contains language to the effect that it covers sales agreements entered into after the expiration of the term of the agent's employment contract with respect to any recordings (whenever made) relating to a creative property or package program which is the subject of any sale agreement existing at the time the agent is engaged or entered into during the term of the agent's agreement. Unless I'm reading this wrong, it seems to mean that if there is a sales agreement entered into after the agent no longer represents you, for a recording relating to a creative property which was sold before you hired the agent, then the agent is entitled to his commission. Now that just doesn't make any sense at all, does it?

The payment provisions are followed by a sentence which reads:

> Said percentages are to be paid to you (the agent) whether or not any sale agreement has been procured or accomplished as a result of your efforts and whether or not any sale agreement shall become effective, or compensation thereunder become due and payable, before, during, or after the term hereof.

Doesn't that mean that the agent is entitled to a commission even if not as a result of his efforts, and even if the agreement is effective and the compensation becomes due and payable after the term of his agreement with you? In other words, your agency agreement might run out, and without your agent's knowledge or assistance you might sell a recording relating to a creative property on which he might claim a commission. That is what the agreement says. Or at least that is what I think it says. I also think this is probably intended to mean that if the agent sells a package program for you, he will also receive commissions on any related recordings, no matter when sold. At the very least, this sentence is most ambiguous. If it is intended to apply to any sales during the term the agent represents you, I am confident that it is easier to say this without using the kind of language which might be interpreted to mean that the agent can claim a commission on anything you do no matter when sold and no matter when payment is made to you. This fuzzy language is in a contract used by one or more of the large agencies.

The agreement says that the agent represents you strictly

as the creator and owner of creative properties and package programs and will not obtain employment for the packager. You will remember that this avoids the necessity of the representative's having an employment agency license, although in this instance, the agency using this contract is in fact licensed.

The one provision of this agreement I do like states that the agent is not representing the packager with respect to his entering into this agreement and that the packager is free to utilize independent legal counsel in connection with his rights and obligations under this agreement. I think it is important for agents to call the client's attention to this provision, for it is just one small provision in a very thick and lengthy contract, and if the client manages to read to that part of the agreement and understands what everything else before it says, he probably will have by then gone to a lawyer of his own accord.

AGENCY AND ARTIST'S MANAGER CONTRACTS

One of the agency form contracts is labeled "Agency and Artist's Manager," and when you inquire of the agent what this is all about and what it's for, you may be told that this is to give him the right to represent you throughout the world. He probably won't go on to say, but I will, that it not only gives him representation of you throughout the world, but that it is also very broad and covers a lot of things that aren't covered by the other standard union-approved forms.

When you sign this form, you employ the agent as your

sole and exclusive representative, manager, and agent in the entertainment, literary, and related fields throughout the world. The contract not only covers your services in the entertainment, literary, and related fields, but also covers the sale, lease, license, use, or other disposition of all material disposed of in the entertainment, literary, or related fields owned or later acquired by you. Of course "entertainment, literary, and related fields" are very broadly defined in the same way that "services" and "material" are broadly defined in the other contracts we discussed. It would be pointless to quote the definition here. You can well imagine from our discussion of the other agreements the kind of language that is used. Thus in addition to giving the agent representation throughout the world, the contract also gives him representation in almost everything imaginable.

Again, I must repeat, I have no objection at all to an actor or writer granting his agent the authority to represent him in all ways in all parts of the world, provided, and this I believe is the important thing, that the actor or writer knows what he is doing. I do, however, strongly object to an agent's non-disclosure of what some of these agreements cover. It is more than misleading, as sometimes happens, just to say this gives the agent world-wide representation. I object to any misrepresentation, whether by non-disclosure or partial disclosure or otherwise.

AGENCY INDUSTRIAL FILMS CONTRACTS

Some agencies have a contract covering the disposition

of industrial films. The agent is paid 10% of the gross compensation on any contract in connection with the disposition of an industrial film. Industrial films are broadly defined to include all non-theatrical motion pictures, such as industrial motion pictures, motion pictures made for a profit or for a non-profit organization, all documentary, training, educational, informational, promotional, selling, advertising, public relations, house, institutional, and similar motion pictures, tapes, and recordings, with or without sound and no matter how recorded.

AGENCY MOTION PICTURE PACKAGES CONTRACTS

Some agents also have a separate agreement covering motion picture packages which includes contracts for financing, production, distribution, or other disposition of photoplays.

The agreement has a blank which is filled in to set forth the photoplays specifically covered by this agreement. The agreement also covers other photoplays which will be produced or created in which the signing party has a substantial interest.

A photoplay is very broadly defined to include not only the motion picture, but the literary property on which the motion picture may be based.

The agent receives 10% of the gross compensation and other consideration received with respect to any financing, production, or distribution agreements, pursuant to any agreements relating to the sale, lease, license, distribution, or other disposition of any such photoplay or photoplays; agreements relating to the sale, lease, license, or other disposition of the literary properties upon which the motion picture may be based and arising out of any renewals, extensions, or modifications of any of the previously-mentioned agreements.

This is the language used in the agreement. Stated simply, this means that the agent will receive his commission on all receipts from the movie from all sources (such as receipts from theatrical or television presentation, or publishing of the screenplay, or funds from the granting of the right to make a stage musical based on the motion picture) at any time.

GENERAL MANAGER, PERSONAL MANAGER, AND EXCLUSIVE MANAGER

A manager not bound by the restriction of a union franchise, which would mean the restriction of a pre-negotiated contract, may do as much or as little for his client and may charge as much or as little as the parties agree to. In fact, in some instances, managers have a large interest in the client because of money they advanced as a loan or even sometimes as a gift. This is done to make certain that the actor has enough to eat so that he will stay in the business rather than end up selling shoes or banging a typewriter.

There are various labels for a manager, such as "personal manager," "general manager," "exclusive manager," "my goddam manager," and "my beautiful manager."

"Exclusive manager" usually refers to a manager who handles concert, opera, and ballet performers or stars. "Exclusive" means you use only that manager; it does not mean that he represents only you. A "general" or "personal" manager may also handle concert, ballet, and opera stars, and any manager—in fact, most—are "exclusive," even if not so labeled. "Goddam" and "beautiful" we all understand.

I would like to say that the management contract which is entered into is a result of negotiation between the actor and the manager. I would like to, but I can't, for such is not often the case. Frequently there is little or no negotiation, for the actor is uninformed and rarely consults anyone. When the actor does consult someone to negotiate the management contract for him, the result is usually different from the way it was originally planned.

One thing a manager legally cannot do is find employment for the actor. As was previously discussed, an exclusive manager may not find employment for a client, but can find an engagement for a client who is an independent contractor, as distinguished from an employee. The manager may arrange to promote the actor's career, give him business tips, manage all the details of his career, and even look after his financial investments and personal life. Most often the manager's fee will range between 10% and 33-1/3% of the actor's gross earnings. If an agent is required to obtain bookings for an actor, then the percentage payable to the agent may or may not be deducted from the manager's share, depending upon the percentage that the manager is entitled to receive, and on the respective bargaining power (if in fact the actor has or knows he has any bargaining power) between the parties.

CONFERENCE OF PERSONAL MANAGERS AND OTHER MANAGEMENT CONTRACTS

I suspect that many of the personal managers were just as concerned as some of the other people in the industry about some of the unscrupulous methods of some managers when they got together to counteract these methods and organized an association known as the Conference of Personal Managers. The Conference has both an East Coast and a West Coast branch. Its purpose is to set forth ethical standards for its members, and to encourage and assist members. The unspoken objective, I am sure, is to erase the bad image which has been projected by what must be a few notorious personal managers, and to create a healthy image.

The Conference of Personal Managers has prepared a standard management contract, and although managers need not use it, I assume that most members of the Conference do. The agreement provides that you are engaging the manager to advise, counsel, and direct you in the development of your artistic and theatrical career. The number of years of the engagement is left blank, to be filled in at the signing of the agreement. There is a list of general duties the manager is supposed to perform, which can be summarized as "advise and counsel." The manager may, at his discretion, do the following:

1. Approve and permit any publicity and advertising.

2. Approve and permit the use of the artist's name and photograph, voice, likeness, etc., for advertising and publicity.
3. Execute contracts and agreements for the performer's services.
4. Collect money belonging to the performer, and endorse and cash checks.
5. Retain the manager's fee from the monies collected.
6. Engage and discharge agents, managers, and employment agencies.

The manager is not obligated to lend the performer any money, but if he does so, the performer agrees to repay it promptly, and of course the manager may deduct any such loans from monies belonging to the performer which come into the manager's hands.

The performer, on the other hand, agrees:

1. To devote himself to his career.
2. To use such agents as required.
3. To advise the manager of all employment possibilities.

The agreement states that the manager is not representing you exclusively, but may represent other people.

The amount of the compensation, like the term of the contract, is left blank, to be filled in at the time the contract is prepared.

As to what one pays one's manager, I am convinced that the percentage is less important than what the manager accomplishes for the performer. If you pay your manager

10% and he does nothing to assist you, you are paying him too much. If he takes as much as 33-1/3% of your earnings and makes you a big star earning large quantities of money, then you have not paid him too much. I always suggest to my actor and actress clients that it would be very nice if their agents and/or managers became rich as a result of their work. If your manager or agent does, think how well you will be doing.

The percentage payable to the manager covers all of your activities in the entertainment, amusement, musical, recording, and publishing industries, including all sums for the use of your artistic talents and the results and proceeds thereof. The definition is broad enough to include anything you may do, as it even includes your likeness and talents for purposes of advertising and trade. If you become famous and there is a chain of beauty shops franchised with your name, the money received by you from the use of your name would thus be included. The gross receipts also include any sums paid for a package TV or radio program, whether it is earned or received directly or indirectly by you or by your heirs. If the performer becomes a stockholder in a corporation and the corporation then engages his services, then the manager's percentage is applied to all of the benefits the performer receives from the corporation whether in the form of cash or the right to buy stock.

The agreement does provide that if you die, any gross monies earned after your death from contracts and agreements which were substantially negotiated prior to your death shall be payable at the rate of 50%.

An arbitration clause is included, and there is a provision that if the manager is an individual he may assign the agreement to a corporation or partnership if he is still involved in it as a stockholder or partner. There is a similar assignment provision if the manager is a partnership or corporation.

There are two parts of the contract in bold type. I think the boldness of the type is significant. It says:

> It is clearly understood that you are not an employment agent or theatrical agent or artists' manager; that you have not offered or attempted or promised to obtain, seek or procure employment or engagements for me, and that you are not obligated, authorized, licensed, or expected to do so.

The other paragraph in bold type states in effect that your manager is not an "artist's manager," but is acting solely as a personal manager, and that the manager is not licensed as an artists' manager under the labor code of California or as a theatrical employment agency under the general business law of the State of New York. This bold type is significant in pointing out the distinction between an agent, who is licensed by the Department of Licenses, and a manager, who is not.

I do believe that this standard personal manager's contract is a step in the right direction. I could more easily give it my unqualified approval if I knew the length of time the performer signs for, and the amount of the compensation.

I am also somewhat troubled by the fact that the agreement permits the manager, without the actor's approval, to sign any agreement obligating the actor to perform. The manager under this agreement may, at his sole discretion, sign the actor to a part obligating the actor to perform at any time, at any place, or may sell a writer's literary or musical materials to anyone at any price.

It is not unreasonable for the actor to insist that any such commitments first have his approval, and that any obligations be signed only after he gives his okay. The manager often insists that he isn't going to do anything that isn't good for the actor's professional career, and this may very well be so; but if the manager cannot convince the actor that what he wants him to do is good for him and that he should do it, then the actor ought to have the last word as to what he does.

I know that the actor–manager relationship is based on personal confidence and trust, but I really feel that this same confidence and trust could still exist with a contract which at least obligates the manager to obtain the actor's approval before obligating the actor. I am sure that because the contract says the manager must advise and counsel, there is a legal obligation to keep the actor informed. I am just naive enough to think that the actor or writer is entitled to be even more than informed. I also believe that he should have some say-so concerning what work he does or to whom his creations are sold.

There are many other contract provisions included in some personal management contracts, although they are not part of the Conference's standard contract. The manager's contract may provide that he is to be reimbursed for all expenditures made by him on behalf of the actor. If the actor has advice in negotiating his contract with his manager, he may insist that the word "reasonable" be inserted to limit the expenditures, and may further insist that all expenditures on behalf of the actor must first be approved by the actor. For an example, it is not unreasonable for an actor to want to approve of his manager's spending money to travel across the country and spend time in another city at the actor's expense, even though it is for the actor's career that the manager does this. I am not suggesting that any such expenditures are not warranted, but rather that such expenditures might better be authorized by the actor who will pay for them than by the manager who will be enjoying their benefits.

Some management contracts provide that all advances to the actor, or expenditures made on his behalf, must be repaid to the manager, whereas other contracts will provide that such advances and expenditures need only be repaid from monies earned by the actor as a performer or creator in the performing arts. An actor should make certain if he must repay such items either from theatre earnings or otherwise that the agreement provides that repayment may be spread out over a period of time, so that there will always be some income to the actor from his earnings. Otherwise, it is conceivable that if a performer doesn't obtain work for some length of time, when he finally is employed, his first two months' earnings (or more) might go to reimburse the manager immediately. The manager should not be entitled to repayment in one big chunk to the detriment, inconvenience, and hunger of the artist.

The Conference standard contract, incidentally, would permit the manager to reimburse himself for any advances to the performer from all sums received without regard to spreading the repayment over a period of time. Presumably, since the purpose of the advance was to keep the client going, it is assumed the manager will not later defeat this purpose by keeping all the client's receipts at one time.

It should also be noted that the Conference standard form does not specifically mention expenditures on behalf of the performer; however, the other powers granted would certainly permit expenditures and reimbursement. Under that contract, the manager can approve advertising, hire agents, sign contracts for the actor, etc. The Conference form does, however, specifically provide that if the manager (at his discretion) is required to travel for the performer's business, it will be done after arrangements for costs and expenses of such travel. This would appear to imply that the arrangements must be made between the actor and manager, but why the agreement doesn't say this, I do not know. The way the contract is worded, the manager could travel for the artist after "arranging" for costs in one of many ways (some preferable to others). All that is required by the contract is an "arrangement" for costs. This interpretation is especially possible in view of the granting to the manager of authority to travel "in your discretion." The language of the contract covering these travel expenses is not exactly what I would prefer.

Some personal management contracts also provide that the personal manager has a power of attorney to do what he wishes with the actor's money. It is conceivable that a star will become so busy that he will not have time to collect his money, deposit it, pay the bills, and invest what's left, and this is, of course, one of the possible functions that a manager can perform. However—and this is a big however—the manager should be qualified to do so. If the actor does not have this confidence in the manager, he can still limit the manager's authority to invest his money only with the actor's approval, just as we previously mentioned that the actor may wish to limit the manager's spending money on behalf of the actor.

EMPLOYMENT CONTRACTS

EMPLOYMENT CONTRACTS

Having engaged an agent or a personal manager, or not having hired an agent or a personal manager, with a little bit of luck you will have a job, and a different kind of agreement must be signed with the person or company that has hired you. The following discussion includes some of the standard union contracts used. Remember that the union contracts set forth minimum terms, and that there is nothing to prevent an actor from getting more if he can. Also bear in mind that the terms discussed are the barest outline of each contract, and that to discuss all of these agreements in detail would require several volumes.

ACTORS' EQUITY ASSOCIATION
EMPLOYMENT CONTRACTS

There are three standard Actors Equity Association contracts used for a Broadway production, and a standard contract which is used off-Broadway. There are also different contracts used in summer stock, repertory, and other special situations.

The three basic Broadway contracts are:

A standard minimum contract for principal actors.
A standard minimum contract for chorus.
A standard minimum run-of-the-play contract.

The first two are almost identical with just a few minor differences.

The Actors Equity contracts are very simple one-page documents; however, each agreement states that all of the provisions contained in the basic agreement between Equity and the League of New York Theatres, as well as the Equity rules, are part of the agreement, just as if they were set forth at length in the agreement. Most actors are familiar with the Equity rules which are contained in a small 80-page pamphlet put out by the organization.

There are different salary rates set forth for actors and for stage managers. Since June 2, 1968, the rehearsal payments are the same as the minimum salary. Since that date, there is also provision for a cost-of-living increase so that for the year which ends May 31, 1971, although the minimum salary is $155 weekly, the total weekly minimum pay with the cost-of-living increase included comes to $164.55; the road minimum is $205, which with the cost-of-living increase comes to $217.50.

An actor must be paid rehearsal money for at least four weeks for a dramatic production, and at least five weeks for a musical production.

The chorus may be paid extra under certain circumstances, and there are detailed provisions in the rules covering televising, recording, show album, and motion pictures. There are also detailed rules governing the number of performances, rehearsal hours and recesses, and overtime payment for rehearsals and for travel.

The standard minimum contracts for principals and chorus both provide that the actor will be paid a minimum of two weeks' salary. This salary must be paid after the date of the first public performance or the opening date specified in the contract, whichever first occurs.

The standard run-of-the-play contract is distinguished from the standard minimum contracts in that the actor under the run-of-the-play contract is guaranteed a minimum of two weeks' employment during each theatrical season contracted for. The producer employs the actor for a certain number of seasons (conditioned, of course, on the show's running).

If the contract is for more than one season, the actor must be paid a minimum of two weeks' employment for each season contracted unless notice is given, as provided in the contract. If notice is delivered together with payment for all of the seasons contracted after the second season, then the producer does not have to pay the guarantee for the second season.

It is possible to convert a standard contract to a run-of-the-play contract if done in accordance with the contract provisions. It is also possible to convert a chorus contract to a six-month run-of-the-play contract, and there is provision for extending a six-month run-of-the-play contract.

There are detailed provisions on termination of the various kinds of contracts, and specific provisions covering juvenile actors, understudies, layoffs, abandonment of the play, billing, credits, clothes and makeup, photographs, supper clubs, etc.

The off-Broadway contract provides that the minimum paid to actors increases as the weekly gross box office receipts increase. The figures are as follows:

Weekly Gross Box Office Receipts	Salary
Under $4500	$ 75
$4500–5500	80
$5500–6500	90
$6500–7500	100
$7500–8500	115
$8500–9000	135
$9000–9500	145
Over $9500	150

If an actor has completed 44 weeks of employment—not necessarily consecutive employment—in a show which grosses below $8500 per week, then the actor will be paid an additional $7.50 per week. This is intended to compensate actors in long-running productions in small houses where they cannot take advantage of the pay raises which occur as the gross box office receipts increase.

It is now possible to sign an off-Broadway actor for a limited run-of-the-play contract or for up to 9 months, whichever is shorter, provided that the actor is paid a minimum of $150 each week. Unless an actor is signed for a run-of-the-play contract for up to 9 months, the actor may leave the production upon 2 weeks' notice. The producer likewise may terminate an actor's employment upon 2 weeks' notice. An actor need only give 1 week's notice if he is leaving to take other, more remunerative employment in the entertainment industry. At the same time, the producer need only give 1 week's notice to terminate the employment if the show is closing and all of the actors' contracts are being terminated.

Since there are some theatres outside the area defined as the Broadway area which are in excess of 299 seats, and there are some in the Broadway area with less than 299 seats, there is the possibility of a contract being negotiated with Equity which provides special terms for these theatres which are neither Broadway nor off-Broadway as strictly defined. The terms of each such special Equity contract vary depending upon the size of the theatre, the location of the theatre, and such similar provisions.

SCREEN ACTORS GUILD CODIFIED
BASIC AGREEMENT

The Screen Actors Guild has a Codified Basic Agreement which specifically covers theatrical motion pictures and is read together with the other specific agreements. Of course, theatrical motion pictures are no longer shown only in theatres and in many instances end up on the television screen. The agreement says that a motion picture need not be on film to be subject to this agreement, and that whether it is on tape or otherwise, it is no less a motion picture.

The Codified Basic Agreement incorporates 172 pages, most of which are completely filled with fine single-spaced type. It would be impossible to discuss this agreement in any detail without either reproducing the agreement, which is pointless, or requiring many more than 172 pages. Suffice it to say that the Basic Agreement covers in great detail all provisions applicable to the production of a theatrical motion picture.

There are separate documents containing specific provisions for dubbing, for television films, and for industrial films, which are to be read together with the Codified Basic Agreement. There are also specific agreements applicable to New York extra players. Each of these agreements has specific terms and conditions covering employment in these various areas and sets forth the rate of pay and all of the conditions surrounding such work. The commercials agreement is independent of the Codified Basic Agreement, but the other specific agreements are not.

Actors in theatrical motion pictures which are now used on television are paid for television use in accordance with the Basic Agreement. There are different provisions covering motion pictures which were made between January 31, 1960 and January 31, 1966, and those which commenced principal photography after January 31, 1966, as well as specific provisions covering theatrical motion pictures which commenced principal photography prior to February 1, 1960.

Day players, that is, those employed by the day (at a minimum of $120 per day) other than as extras, stunt men, singers, or professional airline pilots, are paid differently from free-lance players whose weekly guaranteed payment is $1,500 per week or less and who are guaranteed less than $25,000 per picture (minimum of $420 per week). There are separate provisions covering free-lance players whose weekly guarantee is more than $1,500 per week and who are guaranteed less than $25,000 per picture (minimum of course is $1,500 per week) , and specific provisions covering multiple picture players who receive less than $1,500 per week and are guaranteed less than $25,000 per picture (minimum of $420 per week) . A multiple picture player is a player who is employed for two or more pictures per year who works non-exclusively. The contract may actually be for more than a year as long as the contract provides that the player does at least two pictures during any yearly period.

There are also separate terms covering a contract player whose weekly guaranteed salary is $1,500 or less per week (minimum for other than "beginners" is $360 if 10 to 19 weeks' employment is guaranteed, and $300 per week if 20 or more weeks' employment is guaranteed; minimum for beginners is $162 per week during the first 6 months, and $180 per week for the second 6 months) , and separate provisions for contract players whose weekly guaranteed salary is in excess of $1,500 per week (minimum is $1,500 per week) ; multiple picture players receiving more than $1,500 per week (minimum is $1,500 per week) or who are guaranteed $25,000 or more per picture; and players employed under "deal contracts" (a deal player is one employed for one or more pictures at a guaranteed salary of $25,000 per picture) or otherwise, who are guaranteed $25,000 or more per picture.

Professional singers employed by the day are covered separately (minimums: soloists and duets, $140 per person per day; groups of 3 and 4, $120 per person per day; groups of 5 or more, $100 per person per day) , as are professional singers contracted by the week at $1,500 or less per week (minimums: soloists and duets, $425 per person; groups of 3 or 4, $385 per person; groups of 5 or more, $350 per person) . The contractor is paid an additional sum.

Stunt players employed by the day (minimum $120 per day) and stunt players employed by the week at $1,500 or less per week (minimum is $450 per week) each have their own contractual provisions, as do stunt players employed by the week at more than $1,500 per week (minimum is $1,500 per week) . There are also separate contract provisions for stunt players employed under term contracts (minimum is $360 per week if guaranteed 10 out of 13 weeks' employment, and $300 per week if guaranteed 20 out of 26 weeks' employment) , and for airplane pilots (minimum studio rates are $162 daily and $450 weekly; minimum location rates are $210 daily, including taxiing and flying, and $450 weekly) . A pilot employed by the week is paid an extra $138 per day if he flies or taxis a plane.

The terms in each classification cover minimum wages or salary, working periods, rest periods, meal periods, wardrobe fittings, publicity, interviews, illness of player, rehearsal times, travel time, holiday and night work rates, and the like.

There are detailed provisions in the contract for free-lance players whose weekly guaranteed salary is $1,500 or less per week and who are guaranteed less than $25,000 per picture, covering travel time, with definitions of the studio zone, location and overnight location, near location, distant location, place of reporting and dismissal. Travel time is generally work time; however, no more than eight hours in any twenty-four hours of travel time will be counted.

There are provisions covering intervening time between dismissal and travel, travel on the seventh day, furnishing of travel and lodging going to and from location, computation of overtime caused by travel time, travel time to distant locations at the beginning or end of a player's term of employment, transportation and travel time on overnight locations to or from hotel or camp, travel to or from overnight locations on boat or train where sleeping accommodations are provided, overnight trip to or from location, travel on holidays and Sundays, travel pursuant to recall for added scenes, engagement of actors from other areas, and other general provisions covering travel time.

In this one contract alone, the provisions I have just mentioned covering travel time consume three and one-half large pages of single-spaced type. This surely illustrates the extent of the detail covered by the various SAG contracts.

Similarly, the day player's contract has three and three-fourths pages of travel time provisions. The contract players with a guaranteed salary in excess of $1,500 per week or multiple picture players receiving more than $1,500 per week or guaranteed more than $25,000 per picture, or players employed under deal contracts or otherwise, or who are guaranteed more than $25,000 per contract, have extended and detailed provisions in their contracts covering the player's work week, the studio five-day week, overnight location work, work on holidays, Saturdays, and Sundays. Reference is made to Saturday and Sunday work on a single picture engagement where the guaranteed compensation to the player is less than $50,000.

1967 SCREEN ACTORS GUILD TELEVISION AGREEMENT

This agreement specifically covers employment for television motion pictures, and although similar to the terms of the Codified Basic Agreement covering theatrical motion pictures, it has separate provisions for:

1. Standard non-commercial billboards, and standard non-commercial openings, closings, lead-ins to and lead-outs from commercials, bridging lines, and musical signatures intended for use with three or more episodes on a designated series of television entertainment films.

   Minimum compensation on camera for 1 day is $420, and $120 for each additional day. The same fees apply off-camera for other than singers. Off-camera, soloists and duets receive $324 each per day; groups of 3 to 4 receive $306 each per day; and groups of 5 or more receive $282 per day. All off-camera singers receive $120 for each additional day. If the film is intended for use with one episode of a designated series of television films, the daily rate is $120.

2. Actors' television motion picture day players' con-

tract which states the following minimum daily rates:

Day player—stunt man	$120
Singers—solo and duets	130
Singers—groups of 3 or 4	115
Singers—groups of 5 or more	100
Mouthing (1–16)	90
Mouthing (17 or over)	75
Airplane pilots—studio (includes taxiing)	162
Airplane pilots—location (includes taxiing and flying)	210

3. Actors' television motion picture minimum three day contract (continuous three days):
   For a single one-half hour or one-hour picture

Actors and singers	$306
Stunt men	330

   For a single one and one-half hour picture

Actors, singers, and stunt men	$360

4. Actors' television motion picture free-lance weekly contract whose minimums are:

Actors and singers	$420
Stunt men	450
Pilots	450
Pilots' adjustment for taxiing and flying	138

The day player is paid for a minimum of eight hours of work per day, and there is provision for additional compensation for overtime. The day player's contract provides that he is entitled to a 12-hour consecutive rest period from the time he is finally dismissed until his next call, whether the next call is for makeup, wardrobe, hairdressing, or any other purpose.

The day player is entitled to one rest period in each week consisting of 36 consecutive hours with certain exceptions which are set forth in the contract. If a player is given 2 consecutive days off during a studio work week, the 36-hour consecutive rest period is increased to 58 consecutive hours, which under certain circumstances might be reduced to 56 hours. The rest period provisions also allow for certain exceptions.

The Screen Actors Guild Television Agreement also provides a different fee arrangement for:

1. Multiple pictures on weekly contracts:

    Stunt men and pilots weekly minimum for 1/2 and 1 hour programs — $450

    Stunt men and pilots weekly minimum for 1-1/2 hour programs — 500

    All others weekly minimum for 1/2 and 1 hour programs — 282

    All others weekly minimum for 1-1/2 hour programs — 332

2. Series contracts for 1/2 hour programs:

    Minimum per episode with 13 episodes guaranteed — $420

    Minimum per episode with less than 13 episodes guaranteed — 480

3. Series contracts for 1 hour programs:

    Minimum per episode with 13 episodes guaranteed — $504

Minimum per episode with less than 13 episodes guaranteed   564
4. Series contracts for 1-1/2 hour programs:
Minimum per episode with 13 episodes guaranteed $672
Minimum per episode with less than 13 episodes guaranteed   762
5. Series contracts with a guarantee of more than 13 episodes in the first employment period:
Minimum per episode $420 or $504 or $762 depending on the length of the episode; and there are other specific provisions.
6. Term contracts, which are for a term of at least 10 out of 13 weeks for television or theatrical motion picture or both:
Beginners' weekly minimums:
First 6 months $162
Second 6 months   180
All others' weekly minimums:
If guaranteed 10 but no more than 10 weeks $360
If guaranteed 20 or more weeks   300

The television contracts provide that the salary paid for services in a television motion picture constitutes payment in full for the telecasting of the motion picture once in each city in the United States and Canada. There are detailed provisions covering reruns, and equally detailed provisions covering additional compensation for theatrical rights.

NEW YORK EXTRA PLAYERS AGREEMENT

The SAG New York Extra Players Agreement specifically covers extra players in motion pictures based in New York and in those not based in New York. If the studio is situated within fifty miles of Columbus Circle, the movie is New York-based, and this agreement applies within a radius of three hundred air miles from Columbus Circle. If the motion picture is made by a studio situated outside of the New York metropolitan area (fifty air miles from the center of Columbus Circle), then it is not based in New York and the agreement applies within a radius of 75 air miles of Columbus Circle.

Newsreels and travelogues are exempted from the operation of this agreement, and children under fourteen are excluded from certain paragraphs.

The agreement sets forth minimum wage scales based on a daily rate and a weekly rate. (The contract also provides for waiver of payment under certain conditions, but the waiver procedure outlined must be carefully followed to take advantage of the waiver.) There are special provisions covering waivers of crowd work, and undirected scenes, which includes crowds at public events. Undirected street scenes, and industrial operations, technical or complicated machinery, armed forces personnel, and television audience participation shows are also specifically treated in connection with waivers. For an example, the contract states that it will liberally grant waivers for the photography of persons actually operating technical or complicated equipment or machinery.

There are extra payments provided for hazardous work and for wet work. As with some of the other contracts, body makeup, skull caps, hairgoods, and wardrobe allowances are discussed, as well as costume fittings, rehearsals, special business, automobile, trailer, and skate allowance.

The work day is defined, the work week is defined, and overtime, Saturday, Sunday, and holiday payments are discussed in detail. For an example, a daily employee is guaranteed one day's pay—that is, eight hours—subject to cancellation for unusual circumstances, such as illness of the principal cast, fire, flood, or other catastrophe, government regulations, and weather conditions under certain circumstances. The work week or payroll week for daily employees is the established payroll week of the producer, consisting of seven consecutive calendar days, starting on Saturday, and for weekly employees the payroll week starts with the employee's first day of employment. Extra players who report on a "weather permitting" call must be paid one-half day's pay if they are not used for which the producer is entitled to hold the player for up to four hours. An extra player receives one-fourth of his pay for each additional two hours or fraction thereof during which he is held by the producer. There are specific provisions detailing exactly what the extra may or may not do if he is held under such circumstances. A "weather permitting" call must specify the kind of weather that will permit the filming.

The contract sets forth provisions covering sanitation,

payment requirements, hiring of extras, the New York studio zone, transportation, traveling expenses and accommodations, and the like. Television commercials are not covered by this agreement, but are covered by the specific SAG New York Extras Television Commercials Agreement.

COMMERCIALS

At first blush one would think that the American Federation of Television and Radio Artists would be the union controlling television commercials. Strangely enough, the Screen Actors Guild and AFTRA both have commercials contracts. However, I would hazard a guess that a much larger percentage of TV commercials are controlled by SAG than by AFTRA. At any rate, there is no dispute between the two unions.

Technically, tape commercials are under AFTRA's jurisdiction. However, SAG not only controls film commercials but also commercials prepared by producers who are film oriented, whether made on film or on tape.

In all events, one should bear in mind that there are two controlling unions.

SCREEN ACTORS GUILD
COMMERCIAL CONTRACT

Although, as was stated, the Codified Basic Agreement of 1967 of the Screen Actors Guild is the basic agreement, the Commercials Contract, unlike the other specific contracts, is separate and read independently of the Basic Agreement.

Under the Screen Actors Guild commercials contract, a person doing a commercial is paid (1) a minimum compensation daily base fee (on-camera) or session fee (off-camera) and thereafter is paid (2) for the use of the commercial. The use payments are different for a "wild spot" and for a commercial for "program use." There is also (3) a fee known as a "holding fee," which in effect reserves the commercial for the sponsor during a fixed cycle and binds the performer exclusively to the product.

The minimum payments for an eight-hour day are different for "principal players" and for "group singers." The session fee was recently raised for principal players to $136 for on-camera work and $102 for off-camera work.

The daily base pay (that is, payment for on-camera work in making the commercial) is also considered payment for the first commercial made for one designated advertiser. The player must be paid the applicable additional base pay minimum fee for each commercial in excess of one. The actor must be paid no later than twelve working days after the services are rendered and the producer must notify the player of the total number of commercials made.

USE PAYMENTS
WILD SPOTS

A commercial is called a "wild spot" if it is broadcast by non-interconnected single stations and (1) is used independently of any program or (2) is used on local participating programs. All other uses are program uses.

Payments for use of wild spots are for an unlimited use within a cycle of 13 consecutive weeks. Use during additional 13 consecutive week cycles may be obtained by paying the player the applicable fee. It must be borne in mind that since a wild spot may be playing in more than one city, the 13-week cycle is computed in each city. However, in no event can the 13-week cycle extend for more than 17 weeks after the first use of the commercial in any city.

The payment for use of a wild spot varies from city to city, and use in a larger city requires a larger payment. Each city is weighted and given a unit depending upon its size. Larger cities have a larger unit weight. For an example: Detroit has a 3-unit weight and Philadelphia has a 5-unit weight. Cities like Baltimore and Cleveland are each weighted at 2. At contract negotiations between the union and the producers' association, the weights of a particular city may change. The fee for the use of a wild spot is computed by multiplying the total unit weight by the applicable rates. There are different rates for players and for group singers, and different rates for off-camera and on-camera work.

Philadelphia, Boston, Pittsburgh, and 7 one-unit cities would total 17 units. The rates for on-camera work of a principal (not including New York, Chicago, or Los Angeles) would be as follows: 1–5 units, $136 each; 6–10 units, $10 each; 11–20 units, $6.60 each. Thus the player's compensation for a wild spot for unlimited use of an on-camera principal for 13 weeks in these cities would be $136 plus 5 times $10, or $50, plus 7 times $6.60, making a total of $232.20. The rates for New York, Chicago, and Los Angeles are different.

The Screen Actors Guild Commercials Contract form has helpful wild spot payment tables covering the wild spot payments in various cities for on-camera work, off-camera work, principal performers, and group singers. It is a most useful guide in determining payments for wild spot commercial uses.

PROGRAM COMMERCIALS

The compensation for use of "program commercials" is computed differently. If the commercial is to be used in over 20 cities, it is considered a Class A commercial; if it is to be used in from 6 to 20 cities, it is a Class B commercial; and if it is to be used in from 1 to 5 cities, it is a Class C commercial. New York, Chicago, and Los Angeles each counts as 11 cities. A certain fixed amount is paid for the 1st use, the 2nd use, the 3rd use, the 4th–13th uses, the 14th–26th uses, the 27th use, and each use thereafter.

The Class A program use (over 20 cities—each a 13-week cycle) rates for principals are as follows:

	On-Camera	Off-Camera
1st use	$136	$102
2nd use	83	65
3rd–13th uses	63 each	50 each

	On-Camera	Off-Camera
14th–26th uses	25 each	18 each
27th use and thereafter	22 each	16 each

With a guarantee of 13 uses:

On-Camera	Off-Camera
$775, then $52.40 for each of the 14th–18th uses	$610, then $39.40 for each of the 14th–18th uses

The Class A rates for singing groups are not duplicated here, but may be obtained from the Screen Actors Guild.

Class B and Class C have different rates fixed which permit unlimited use in the cities for each 13-week cycle. There is a special New York Class B program rate which is different from the regular Class B program rate. The following rates apply for principals for each 13-week cycle.

	On-Camera	Off-Camera
Class B program use (6–20 cities)	$275	$192
New York Class B program use	335	240
Class C program use (1–5 cities)	172.50	115

For singers, the following rates apply for each 13-week cycle:

Class B program use
(6–20 cities)

	On-Camera	Off-Camera
Groups of 3–4	$214.50	$79.20
Groups of 5–8	189.75	66
Groups of 9 and over	155.25	54

Class C program use
(1–5 cities)

Groups of 3–4	148.50	66
Groups of 5–8	132	55
Groups of 9 and over	108	45

An example of compensation under a Class A commercial use fee is as follows. The first use for a Class A commercial, which would mean use in over 20 cities during a 13-week cycle, would be $136. The second use would be $83. The 3rd–13th uses would be $63 each. The 14th–26th uses would be $25 each, and the 27th and each use thereafter would be $22. Thirteen uses computed in accordance with these rates would mean a payment of $912. However, if the producer wished to guarantee 13 uses, he would pay the performer only $775, which is the guaranteed amount for 13 uses.

In computing the payment for a Class B or Class C commercial, different dollar amounts would be used.

The negotiations in 1969 of the Screen Actors Guild commercials contract ended up with the inclusion of a cost of living clause which provides that if, 18 to 24 months after the contract becomes effective (that is, 18 to 24 months after November 16, 1969, which is the effective date of the contract), the cost of living has increased by 10% or more, there will be an automatic across-the-board increase in all rates for commercials. The guarantees for a certain number of program uses apply only to Class A and not to Class B and C program uses, since the Class B and C rates are for unlimited use during each 13-week period.

PROGRAM OPENINGS AND CLOSINGS

A standard program opening and closing and standard lead-ins and lead-outs for a particular program taken together are considered a single commercial and paid for as such, except that if the commercial is used on different programs, then the openings and closings are paid for as separate commercials.

SIGNATURES OFF CAMERA

There is a specific schedule setting forth payments for "signatures." "Signatures" are off-camera musical themes at the beginning or end or both of television programs. The minimum fees payable to each singer for use of signatures for a 13-week cycle are as follows:

	Class A	Class B	Class C
Solo or Duet	$258.50	$132	to $110
Groups of 3–4	203.50	66	55
Groups of 5–8	176	55	49.50
Groups of 9 and over	144	45	40.50

DEALER COMMERCIALS

There is also a specific rate set forth for "dealer commercials." A dealer commercial is a commercial made and paid for by the manufacturer or distributor of a product or service as distinguished from the dealer in the product or service; it is to be delivered to dealers in the product or service for telecasting by the dealers as a wild spot or as a Class B or C program commercial on local non-network stations, where the station time is contracted by the dealer.

SEASONAL COMMERCIALS

A seasonal commercial can be used for no more than one 13-week cycle plus an additional optional 2 weeks (for which a full cycle payment would be made) and for a limit of 2 consecutive seasons. Seasonal commercials are commercials especially related to a particular season or holiday and are specifically defined because they have special provisions applicable to them. Formerly seasonal commercials were exempt from a holding fee (to be discussed later), but recent negotiations resulted in a contract provision to the effect that a holding fee must be paid after the first season's use. If the fee is not paid, the right to use the commercial expires.

INTEGRATING OF COMMERCIALS INTO DIFFERENT COMMERCIALS

If the photography or sound track of a commercial is integrated into another commercial, the players in the original commercial are entitled to receive the applicable use and reuse payments for it, as well as the payments for the original commercial if it is used. The new commercial would also be subject to the holding fee provisions.

EDITING OF COMMERCIALS

There are specific provisions setting forth what may and what may not be edited without resulting in a new or different separate commercial. The provisions are somewhat detailed. You should know, however, that a new or different commercial may result from the editing.

MAXIMUM PERIOD OF USE AND REUSE

The maximum period during which a commercial may be used is 18 months from the date of first use of a commercial or 18 months from 17 weeks after the beginning of the player's employment, whichever is earlier. The period cannot be extended by editing. There is, however, a provision for automatic extension of the period of use, as long as there is not a default in payment of the reuse fees, and so long as the player does not give written notice within a certain time that he does not wish to extend the use period.

HOLDING FEES

A holding fee is a separate fee paid to a player during fixed cycles for each commercial, which is paid to reserve the right of later use of the commercial. The daily base pay or session fee (the fee for making the commercial) is considered the holding fee for the first fixed cycle. The holding fee is credited against use fees incurred in a 13-week use cycle which commences during the "fixed cycle." Holding fees are now due the date of the first use of a commercial or 17 weeks after the player's beginning of employment, whichever is earlier, and payment must be made within 12 working days after the due date.

The amount of the holding fee is equal to the amount of the daily base pay (on-camera work) or the session fee (off-camera work), whichever is applicable. Unless the player is paid more than the minimum for a base pay or session fee, the holding fee will be either $136 (the on-camera base pay for other than singers) or $102 (the off-camera session fee). Sound complicated? It is, but it's somewhat easier if one remembers the distinction between (1) the daily base pay or session fee, (2) the use fee, and (3) the holding fee, although they are interrelated.

Payment of the daily base pay (or session fee) pays for the first fixed cycle, so at the termination of the first fixed cycle the player must again be paid a holding fee in the amount of the daily base pay (or session fee) for the next fixed cycle. But since holding fees may be credited against use fees, you have the three separate fees, with the complication that:

1. The amount of the base pay or session fee is also the same amount as the holding fee.
2. Payment of the base pay or session fee is payment for the holding fee for the first fixed cycle.
3. Holding fees may be credited against use fees.

A fixed cycle is a period of thirteen weeks computed as set forth in the agreement. There are provisions in the agreement covering commercials advertising the same product and setting forth specific regulations concerning the fixed cycles and holding fees where more than one commercial is made at one time.

Holding fees are not required for (1) off-camera group singers and (2) commercials during a 6-month period in which they are used and paid for as dealer commercials.

The holding fee must be paid or the commercial cannot be used. If there is an inadvertent oversight in the payment, the agreement provides for penalty payments. Although "fixed cycles" (holding cycles) are always consecutive cycles, the cycles of actual use of commercials and the cycles for which use payments must be made need not be consecutive. If this sounds complicated, it sure is. The examples cited in the Commercials contract may help to clarify this and there are a good number of examples set forth in the contract.

EXCLUSIVITY

There are specific provisions set forth in the contract providing for additional payment when the actor is not permitted to accept employment in other commercials either of a competitive or non-competitive nature, and specific provisions defining who may grant exclusivity and who may not.

FOREIGN USE OF COMMERCIALS

There are specific provisions providing for payment for commercials used outside the United States. For an example, the contract provides that a player must receive no less than double the daily base pay or session fee for use of a commercial in the United Kingdom.

THEATRICAL OR INDUSTRIAL EXHIBITION

There are additional fees provided for theatrical or industrial exhibition of commercials.

DATES OF PAYMENT

The payments to each player for the session fee (off-camera) and daily base pay (on-camera) must be made no later than twelve working days after the day or days of employment. Payment of the holding fee is due the date of the first use of the commercial or 17 weeks after the player's beginning of employment, whichever is earlier, and payment must be made within 12 working days thereafter.

Payment to the player for a Class A program commercial must be made no later than 15 working days after the date of each use of the commercial. The players in a Class B and Class C local program commercial must be paid for each cycle of use no later than 12 working days after the date of the first use in the cycle. The players in a wild spot commercial must be paid for each cycle of use no later than 15 days after the date of first use in the cycle, except that adjustments for unit compensation which is non-ascertainable at the time of first use must be paid in full no later than 15 working days after the completion of the cycle.

The contract as mentioned provides for certain discounts if a certain number of uses are guaranteed. However, this discount may be taken only when the guarantee is made prior to the first use and is paid in full within 12 working days after the guarantee is given to the player. Any additional uses above the uses covered by the guarantee payment must be paid no later than 15 working days after each additional use.

Payment is deemed made when received by the player or when posted in the United States mail.

PENALTIES FOR LATE PAYMENT
PENSION, ETC.

The contract provides for penalties for late payments of $2.50 per day up to 30 days, and $5.00 per day after 30 days. After the 30 days the producer is given a grace period of 12 days to make payment and if it is not made the $5.00 per day is retroactive. This could be pretty stiff, so producers and advertising agencies generally make payments on time. An actor must, however, furnish his W–4 form and any other required tax forms or the penalties are not applicable. Penalties are also not applicable if the actor does not return the signed contract promptly or if there is a bona fide dispute as to the amount of the compensation.

The producer must contribute 6-1/2% of all gross compensation to the union for pension and health and welfare plans. Four percent goes to the pension plan and 2-1/2% to the welfare plan, but this may be adjusted by the trustees of SAG.

OVERSCALE PAYMENTS AND GUARANTEES

Payments to a player for his services in excess of the minimum amount provided in the contract cannot be credited by the producer against any reuse fees payable to the player unless the player's individual contract specifically so provides. If a player is guaranteed a fixed sum of money in his contract, he may agree to credit this fixed sum compensation by dividing it up, specifying part for making commercials, part for use fees, and part for holding fees.

112

MULTIPLE AUDITIONS

A player may not be kept for more than an hour on the first audition and an hour on the second audition without payment by the producer. He must be paid his straight time for time in excess of the hour in each audition. In order for the player to be so paid, the call for the interview must be for a definite time and must be given or confirmed by the casting department. The player is also not entitled to such compensation if he is more than five minutes late.

For a third audition, the producer must guarantee payment of a 2-hour call at straight time with payment for excess time at straight time rates in half-hour units. For the fourth and all subsequent auditions, the producer must guarantee payment of a 4-hour minimum call at straight time with payment for excess time at straight time rates in half-hour units. Pension and welfare payments must be made for the third and all subsequent calls.

MISCELLANEOUS

There are specific provisions in the contract covering puppeteers, dubbing by a player, the use of still pictures, stop action photographs, and stunt men.

This is just a very brief consideration of some of the highlights of this agreement which is complicated and covers a wide variety of subjects, including such varied provisions as makeup, hairdress, and wardrobe allowance, meal period, penalties for a violation of a meal period as set forth in the agreement, fittings, wardrobe tests, makeup tests, production conferences, publicity interviews, night work, Saturday and Sunday work, holiday work, weather, rest periods, dressing rooms, et cetera.

NEW YORK EXTRA PLAYERS TELEVISION COMMERCIAL CONTRACTS

The Screen Actors Guild has a specific television commercial agreement for New York extra players. The contract sets forth the daily rate of payment, which payment will differ depending upon the kind of commercial and what the player is engaged to do. In addition, the extras contract effective November 16, 1969, as with the principals' contract, provides for a 5% cost of living increase if the cost of living rises 10% or more between the eighteenth and twenty-fourth months of the contract.

Without examining the contract in any great detail, one should be cognizant of the fact that extra players are paid differently from principals. A producer may select one of three ways of paying the extra player.

1. He may guarantee, at the time the extra player is hired, that the player will be paid the daily rate set forth in the contract plus 100% additional compensation, which is made when the actor is paid his initial wage. This is called a buyout, and permits unlimited use of the commercial without additional payment to the extra player.

2. The producer may alternatively decide to guarantee the extra player when he is hired that he will

be paid the daily rate plus 75% additional compensation, payable at the time he receives his initial wage payment. This payment would cover the initial thirteen-week period of use and a second thirteen-week period of use. The producer would have to pay 35% additional compensation above the daily rate for any use beyond the twenty-six weeks.

3. The producer may decide at the time of hiring to avoid the guarantees noted and may later decide to pay the extra player, in addition to 100% of the compensation for the first thirteen weeks, an amount equal to another 100% for a second thirteen-week period of use. The second payment would be payable after the first thirteen-week cycle. The producer would pay 25% additional compensation for any use beyond twenty- six weeks.

Pension and welfare provisions are applicable to extra players. The extra players contract is fascinating reading. For example, I'll bet you didn't know that an extra riding bareback without stirrups is paid more than someone riding double, but not as much as a jockey riding a race horse in an actual race. I also found it fascinating to learn that an extra actually playing polo would receive almost twice what an extra mounted on a polo pony with a stick in hand would be paid. I need hardly call attention to the fact that an extra riding a camel or an elephant is of course paid more than an extra leading a camel or an elephant. It also goes without saying that the higher the diving board, the more the extra gets paid, and a swimmer is graded upwards in accordance with the work performed.

The contract discusses in detail crowd work, undirected scenes, weekly rates, adjustments, hazardous work, wet and smoke work, body makeup, skullcaps, hair goods, wardrobe maintenance and allowance, costume fittings, interviews, et cetera.

There are also provisions for travel and sanitation, as well as many other useful details.

INDUSTRIALS

The Screen Actors Guild has an Industrial Supplement agreement which specifically covers industrial motion pictures, documentaries, sales motion pictures, educational and training motion pictures—that is, non-theatrical motion pictures. The industrial contract specifically provides a minimum wage for day players of $115 per day until July 21, 1970, and $120 per day after July 21, 1970. The weekly contract for a single picture sets forth a minimum weekly salary of $420.

There are minimum hours provided in the contract. There are also specific provisions covering employment in motion pictures of fifteen minutes or less in length. Stunt men, airplane pilots, and singers are not covered in the Industrial Supplement but in the basic agreement. There are specific provisions for additional compensation for players where the producer desires to acquire television rights and restricted theatrical rights, and a provision for additional compensation for theatrical exhibition.

There are numerous provisions in the Industrial Supplement agreement referring to the basic agreement and the fact that the terms of the basic agreement are incorporated into the Industrial Supplement agreement. It must be borne in mind that the basic agreement as stated is applicable unless there is a conflict with the Industrial Supplement (as with the other specific agreements) and in such event, the provisions of the specific agreement apply.

DUBBING CONTRACTS

There is a specific SAG contract covering dubbing which is read together with the Codified Basic Agreement. The modification agreement specifically covers the employment of actors to dub an English sound track to be used in connection with a foreign-produced motion picture. A daily rate is set forth for the payment of an actor to dub an English sound track.

The rates differ from those for theatrical exhibition (which includes non-network free television use for a period of seven years; the rate for a single role is $112.50 per day and $135 per day for multiple roles), and from those for television exhibition only (non-network; the rate for a single role is $100 daily, and for multiple roles, $120 daily). The rates differ not only for single and multiple role employment, but also for forty loops or more ($135 for theatrical exhibition, $120 daily for television use only), where an actor may be required to dub only one part. A loop is a section of film which is in the shape of a loop and which is viewed repeatedly to assist the dubber and to accomplish the dubbing.

The normal work day is 7 consecutive hours, exclusive of the 1-hour lunch period; however, there are certain exceptions. Provision is made for overtime payments in excess of the normal workday. It is possible that the daily rate will be reduced if the picture does not meet the standards established for television exhibition. There is provision that if the film is originally intended for television, and the producer later wishes to use it for theatrical exhibition, he must make additional payments to the actors who do the dubbing.

Welfare and pension contributions must of course also be paid. There are specific provisions for additional payments for network television if all payments have been made for the right to exhibit the picture on non-network television. The contract provides that the additional payments are applicable to anyone who acquires title to the picture by any means, such as a purchaser.

This agreement is applicable only to present methods of dubbing, and if new methods are invented or devised, the terms would be negotiated. The agreement provides for penalty payments, for late payments, and makes specific references to incorporating the Codified Basic Agreement into the dubbing contract.

AFTRA
AMERICAN FEDERATION OF TELEVISION AND RADIO ARTISTS

While this is being written, most of the American Federation of Television and Radio Artists Codes of Fair Practice have been renegotiated. The negotiations have been completed and the parties have reached agreement. Although the agreements have not been reduced to writing, there have been some changes in the contracts. The rates hereinafter set forth with respect to each contract are substantially correct. The final figures have not as yet been worked out; however, the figures will not be more than fifty cents off in those few instances where there are differences, since the figures were rounded off to the nearest half dollar.

There are AFTRA agreements covering commercials, network television broadcasting, New York local television broadcasting, phonograph recordings, recordings for filmstrips and slide films, and radio transcriptions, all of which are briefly discussed. There are also AFTRA agreements covering commercial radio, sustaining radio, and staff newsmen, which are applicable to such a small percentage of the shows that they are not discussed here. For example, there is just one network show using live singers to which the commercial radio agreement would be applicable.

COMMERCIALS

The American Federation of Television and Radio

Artists' T.V. Recorded Commercials Contract covers taped commercials used on television. Actually, as was pointed out, SAG and AFTRA get along very well and SAG may have jurisdiction, even though the commercial is taped, if it's made by a producer who commonly works with film. The AFTRA Contract now has provisions identical with the SAG Agreement, in fact the code which covers commercials was jointly negotiated by AFTRA and SAG.

All fees are in the same amount as the SAG fees which were previously discussed. Payments are due to each performer at the exact time provided in the SAG agreement which we discussed previously, and, as in the SAG agreement, there are also penalties for late payments.

NETWORK TELEVISION BROADCASTING

The AFTRA contract for network television broadcasting, like all of the AFTRA agreements, expired November 5. 1969, and was renegotiated. The contract deals with payment to the performers, and a distinction is made between payment for performers on dramatic shows and for performers on other shows, such as announcers, or news shows.

Program fees for principal performers are set forth, as are program fees for performers who speak five lines or less. Program fees for announcers off-camera are detailed, and different payments are provided for more than ten lines and less than ten lines. Chorus singers and group dancers are treated separately, as are specialty acts and sportscasters. Walk-ons and extras have special rates, as do live signature numbers.

In all instances, there is a special arrangement for programs on multiple stations commonly owned. The contract covers rehearsals, minimum daily call, and rest periods; and there is a provision that commercial copy that must be memorized must be in the performer's hands at least twenty-four hours before air time. If there are significant changes or additions during the twenty-four hours before air time, the producer must supply an acceptable prompting device or legible cue cards.

Models are paid the applicable fee for the five lines or less category, except for commercials within programs. Additional compensation of $50 or more must be paid a performer taking part in hazardous action or working under hazardous conditions. If a performer is required to grow a beard or moustache, or to shave his head, he must be paid an additional amount.

The contract provides for the time of payment to the performer and includes a cost of living adjustment.

The rates for principal performers, that is, performers who would speak more than five lines; singing and dancing soloists and duos, and announcers who are on camera regardless of the number of lines, is as follows:

Program Length	Program Fee	Payment Includes Rehearsal Hours Performer / Announcer	
15 minutes or less	$110.00	3	3

Program Length	Program Fee	Payment Includes Rehearsal Hours Performer / Announcer	
over 15 to 30 minutes	$181.50	10	7
over 30 to 60 minutes	$230.00	18	12
over 60 to 90 minutes	$350.00	26	17
over 90 to 120 minutes	$350.00	34	22

Extra rehearsals in excess of the number of hours above set forth are paid for at $9.00 per hour.

The Code contains rates for dramatic shows of multiple performances in one week of fifteen minutes or less; between 15 and 30 minutes; between 30 and 60 minutes; between 60 and 90 minutes and between 90 and 120 minutes. The rates for 15 minutes or less and for 15 and 30 minutes are the only ones here duplicated because multiple performance dramatic shows, such as soap operas, of more than 30 minutes are most rare. These rates are applicable to the performers but not the announcers on the dramatic shows and are restricted to performances in the same show each day within the calendar week.

PROGRAM OF 15 MINUTES OR LESS

Performances per week	Program Fee	Incl. Reh. Hours
1	$110.00	3
2	$206.00	7
3	$301.00	11
4	$396.00	15
5	$493.00	19

The most important rates are those that follow since most soap operas and other dramatic shows to which this would be applicable are 30-minute programs.

PROGRAM OVER 15 TO 30 MINUTES

Performances per week	Program Fee	Incl. Reh. Hours
1	$175.00	10
2	$350.00	16
3	$525.00	22
4	$650.00	28
5	$790.00	34

The extra rehearsal pay in all instances for a multiple performance dramatic show is $9.00 an hour.

The rates for performers and announcers for multiple performance shows other than dramatic shows are as follows:

PROGRAM OF 15 MINUTES OR LESS

Performances per week	Program Fee	Incl. Reh. Hours
1	$110.00	3
2	$204.00	7
3	$286.00	11
4	$341.00	15
5	$396.00	19

PROGRAM OVER 15 TO 30 MINUTES

Performances per week	Program Fee	Incl. Reh. Hours
1	$181.50	10
2	$363.00	16
3	$391.00	22
4	$429.00	28
5	$495.00	34

PROGRAM OVER 30 TO 60 MINUTES

Performances per week	Program Fee	Incl. Reh. Hours
1	$230.00	18
2	$370.00	22
3	$440.00	28
4	$528.00	32
5	$649.00	38

PROGRAM OVER 60 TO 90 MINUTES

Performances per week	Program Fee	Incl. Reh. Hours
1	$290.00	26
2	$419.00	28
3	$506.00	34
4	$638.00	36
5	$814.00	40

PROGRAM OVER 90 TO 120 MINUTES

Performances per week	Program Fee	Incl. Reh. Hours
1	$350.00	34
2	$495.00	36
3	$572.00	40
4	$743.00	40
5	$935.00	40

Extra rehearsal pay is at the rate of $9.00 an hour. There are special provisions applicable to the sixth or seventh performance during one calendar week for news shows only, such as news announcers:

PROGRAM LENGTH

	15 min. Fee / Hours		30 min. Fee / Hours		60 min. Fee / Hours	
6th	$440	23	$539	40	$715	40
7th	$484	27	$575	40	$781	40

90 *min.*			120 *min.*		
Fee	/	*Hours*	*Fee*	/	*Hours*
$ 935		40	$1100		40
$1045		40	$1265		40

The extra rehearsal pay for the sixth and seventh news performance during a week is also $9.00.

There are special rates for performers who speak five lines or less. The rates are as follows:

Program Length	Program Fee	Incl. Reh. Hours
15 minutes or less	$ 67.50	3
over 15 to 30 minutes	$ 85.50	5
over 30 to 60 minutes	$105.00	8
over 60 to 90 minutes	$119.50	10
over 90 to 120 minutes	$136.50	12

The extra rehearsal pay for such performers is also $9.00 an hour.

The program fees payable to announcers off-camera are as follows:

MORE THAN 10 LINES

Program Length	Program Fee	Incl. Reh. Hours
15 minutes or less	$ 70	2
over 15 to 30 minutes	$111	3
over 30 to 60 minutes	$155	4

Program Length	Program Fee	Incl. Reh. Hours
over 60 to 90 minutes	$199	5
over 90 to 120 minutes	$243	6

TEN LINES OR LESS

Program Length	Program Fee	Incl. Reh. Hours
15 minutes or less	$ 70	2
over 15 to 30 minutes	$ 78	3
over 30 to 60 minutes	$ 93	4
over 60 to 90 minutes	$108	5
over 90 to 120 minutes	$124	6

MULTIPLE PERFORMANCES IN ONE CALENDAR WEEK, SAME SHOW

2 performances per week at 1 ¾ times the single rate

3 performances per week at 2 ¼ times the single rate

4 performances per week at 2 ¾ times the single rate

5 performances per week at 3 times the single rate

The extra rehearsal rates are as follows:

(1) All performers other than groups, choruses, walk-ons, extras, hand models and physical demonstrators: $8.00 an hour.

(2) Group Dancers: $7.00 an hour; Chorus Singers: $8.00 an hour.

(3) Walk-ons, Extras, Hand Models and Physical Demonstrators: $5.00 an hour.

There are specific rates set forth in the Code for group dancers. The fees payable vary depending upon the size of the group. There is a specific rate for three performers which is slightly less for four performers which is something less than for five performers, etc. Since most groups use more than eight dancers, there is set forth here only the fees payable to each dancer in a group of eight or more, but one should bear in mind that there are greater fees due if the group is smaller.

15 minutes or less	15 to 30 minutes	30 to 60 minutes	60 to 90 minutes	90 to 120 minutes
$122.00	$193.00	$231.00	$267.00	$300.00

If the program is 15 minutes or less, the fee includes eight hours of rehearsal; 15 to 30 minutes, 20 hours of rehearsal; 30 to 60 minutes, 30 hours of rehearsal; 60 to 90 minutes, 36 hours of rehearsal; and 90 to 120 minutes includes 36 hours of rehearsal.

THE NEW YORK LOCAL TELEVISION BROADCASTING CONTRACT

The New York Local Television Broadcasting Contract

is similar to the network television contract except that there is provision for different rates of pay. For an example, the language of each contract covering warm-ups and after-shows is identical, except that the payment to an actor provided for a network warm-up is considerably more than payment for a New York warm-up. The language covering models is identical. The provisions covering live repeat programs is identical, as are the provisions covering group singers or group dancers, understudies, stand-ins, and dance-ins, multiple programs which are part sustaining and part commercial, notice on multiple performances, hazardous performances, etc.

The New York contract has special provisions covering performers and announcers who appear in more than one commercial announcement and group singers, group dancers, walk-ons, and extras who perform in commercial announcements. The provisions covering doubling in the New York contract are much simpler and less detailed than the network agreement. The definitions in both contracts are identical, such as the definition of a line and the definitions of walk-ons and extras.

PHONOGRAPH RECORDINGS

There is a National Code of Fair Practice covering employment for phonograph recordings which is applicable to all persons performing on a record other than instrumental musicians performing as such. The musicians, of course, would be covered by the musicians' union.

The minimum rates payable are as follows: soloists and

duos must be paid a minimum of $68.00 per person, per hour or per side, whichever is higher, provided however, that if they receive any royalty payment the minimum is then $60.50 per person or per side, whichever is higher.

A side consists of one song or a medley on a single record, the playing time of which does not exceed 3½ minutes.

The amount payable to group singers per person, per hour or per side, whichever is higher, is as follows:

Number of Persons	Fee
3 - 8	$25.00
9 - 16	$20.00
17 - 24	$17.75
25 or more (non-classical)	$15.00
25 or more (classical)	$12.00

Actors must be paid a minimum of $42.00 and narrators and announcers $47.50 per hour or per side, whichever is higher.

All persons in a show who perform on an original cast album must be compensated at the minimums as above set forth but in no event may the fee be less than $145.00 per person, per side or per hour, whichever is greater; however, in the case of off-Broadway musical shows, the minimum is $125.00 instead of $145.00.

Actors (other than for an original cast album) as well as narrators and group singers, must be paid a minimum rate equal to the rate for two sides.

Sound effects artists must be paid a minimum of $42.00 for the first hour and $16.00 for each additional half-hour or part thereof. If the sound effects artist performs vocal sound effects, he is paid at the actors' minimum rate.

RECORDINGS FOR FILMSTRIPS AND SLIDE FILMS

There is a National Code which covers sound recordings for filmstrips or slide films which includes persons speaking, acting or singing, or sound effects used on the record.

The minimum fees payable for a narrator, principal soloist, and duos are as follows:

Length of Recording	Included Session		Minimum Fee
up to 7 minutes	2	hours	$ 75.00
7 to 10 minutes	2	hours	$ 85.00
10 to 16 minutes	2½	hours	$100.00
16 to 24 minutes	3½	hours	$120.00
24 to 32 minutes	3½	hours	$140.00

The minimum fee for supporting performers is $50.00. The supporting performer may perform in two roles for the $50.00 minimum, provided the total number of lines in the two roles does not exceed 15. If the two roles exceed 15 lines, then the supporting performer must be paid an additional $50.00. Group singers, consisting of three or more, must each be paid the minimum fee as follows:

Length of Recording	Included Session		Minimum Fee
up to 7 minutes	2	hours	$40.00
7 to 10 minutes	2	hours	$45.00
10 to 16 minutes	2½	hours	$55.00
16 to 32 minutes	2½	hours	$65.00

| 131

A sound effects artist must be paid a minimum fee of $30.00 for a two hour session and $2.50 for each 15 minutes exceeding two hours.

RADIO TRANSCRIPTIONS

The Radio Transcription National Code applies to all transcriptions for radio which includes transcriptions of shows and commercials. The minimum fees provided for actors are as follows:

Length of Program	Fee Per Person
up to 5 minutes	$22.40
5 to 15 minutes	$24.00
15 to 30 minutes	$40.00
30 to 60 minutes	$56.00

Announcers for transcriptions are paid a minimum as follows:

Length of Program	Fee Per Person
up to 15 minutes	$24.00
15 to 30 minutes	$40.00
30 to 60 minutes	$56.00

The Code sets forth minimum rates payable to singers, signature voices, and dramatized commercials. There are also specific fees set forth for wild spots for an eight consecutive week cycle and for a thirteen consecutive week cycle. The rates vary depending upon the use of the wild spot; that is, whether the wild spot is used in the three major cities (defined as New York, Los Angeles and

Chicago), or the three major cities together with other cities, one major city alone or together with other cities, Chicago or Los Angeles alone or with other cities, New York alone or with other cities, or solely in cities other than the major cities. For example, an actor or announcer whose spot of one minute or less is used for a thirteen week consecutive cycle in the three major cities alone must be paid $93.60 but if it is used in the three major cities plus 1 to 25 other cities the minimum fee is $105.60; the three major cities plus 26 to 100 other cities for this same spot requires a payment of $114.00 and for the three major cities plus 101 or more other cities a payment of $126.00 is required.

A FINAL OBSERVATION

It is hoped that this book will help you to have some idea of the basic relationship between a performer and his agent or manager, and between a performer and his employer. The contracts discussed in this book are, for the most part, involved and complicated. Of course, it is impossible for this book or any other book to answer all the questions you might have about the contracts discussed, so, even if this doesn't give you all the answers, it can, at least, help you pose the questions you should want answered and point some direction in which the answers can be found. If you have any specific questions about any contractual relationship, consult your agent, manager, union representative, or attorney, who should be in a position to answer the questions for you.

Please also bear in mind that the terms of the contracts discussed in this book are likely to change from time to time. As a matter of fact, the off-Broadway employment contract had been renegotiated at the time that this book was written, but the terms were not yet available for publication. You should be conscious of the fact that although the terms may change, in most circumstances the changes will be the kind of thing that you can easily determine such as dollar amount or hourly rates. In most instances the basic contractual obligations are not usually changed that much that often. It is for this reason that an understanding of the rights, duties and obligations which each party has to the other is helpful in creating a kind of an atmosphere that one would hope to work in.

DATE DUE

DEMCO 38-297